WINNER OF THE 2020 YALSA EXCELLENCE IN
YOUNG ADULT NONFICTION AWARD

A *KIRKUS REVIEWS* BEST CHILDREN'S BOOK OF 2019

"Recounting his childhood experiences in sixth grade, [Rex] Ogle's memoir chronicles the punishing consequences of poverty and violence on himself and his family. . . . Balancing the persistent flashes of brutality, Ogle magnificently includes sprouts of hope. . . . [A] fine balance carried by the author's outstanding, gracious writing and a clear eye for the penetrating truth. A mighty portrait of poverty amid cruelty and optimism." —*Kirkus Reviews*, starred review

"With candor and vivid detail, Ogle's debut . . . captures the experience of chronic poverty in the United States. . . . Ogle's emotional honesty pays off in the form of complex characterization and a bold, compassionate thesis." —*Publishers Weekly*, starred review

"Heart-wrenching, timely, and beautifully written, this is a powerful and urgent work. . . . Ogle's story will inspire empathy for the experience of children living in poverty."
—*School Library Journal*, starred review

"Ogle's engrossing narrative is rich in lived experience, offering a window into the ways that poverty can lead to domestic violence and feelings of unworthiness. . . . [T]oo many others will recognize Rex's circumstances as their own." —*Booklist*

FREE
LUNCH

REX OGLE

Norton Young Readers

An Imprint of W. W. Norton & Company
Independent Publishers Since 1923

Free Lunch is a work of nonfiction. Dialogue has been reconstructed to the best of the author's ability. Locations have been altered or invented, and all character names, with the exception of the author's, have been changed, along with certain details of physical description.

For information about permission to reproduce selections from this book, write to Permissions, W. W. Norton & Company, Inc., 500 Fifth Avenue, New York, NY 10110

For information about special discounts for bulk purchases, please contact W. W. Norton Special Sales at specialsales@wwnorton.com or 800-233-4830

Manufacturing by LSC Harrisonburg
Book design by Daniel Lagin Design
Production manager: Julia Druskin

Library of Congress Cataloging-in-Publication Data

Names: Ogle, Rex, author.
Title: Free lunch / Rex Ogle.
Description: New York, NY : Norton Young Readers, an imprint of
   W. W. Norton & Company, [2019] | Audience: Ages: 11–14
Identifiers: LCCN 2019014202 | ISBN 9781324003601 (hardcover)
   Subjects: LCSH: Ogle, Rex—Childhood and youth—Juvenile literature. |
   Poor children—United States—Biography—Juvenile literature. | Hunger—
   Juvenile literature. | School children—Food—Juvenile literature. |
   Middle school students—Juvenile literature.
Classification: LCC HV741 .O35 2019 | DDC 362.7092 [B]—dc23
   LC record available at https://lccn.loc.gov/2019014202

ISBN 978-1-324-01694-6 pbk.

W. W. Norton & Company, Inc., 500 Fifth Avenue, New York, N.Y. 10110
www.wwnorton.com

W. W. Norton & Company Ltd., 15 Carlisle Street, London W1D 3BS

1 2 3 4 5 6 7 8 9 0

This book is for every kid,
whether they pay for their lunch or not.

COUPONS

My stomach growls. This morning, I skipped breakfast, though not 'cause I want to. When Mom steers our old two-door Toyota hatchback into a parking space in front of Kroger, I mumble, "I hate grocery shopping."

"Well, how else are we going to eat?" Mom says.

"Eat what? You never get anything I like."

"When you get a job and start paying for the groceries yourself, you can buy whatever you want."

"I can't get a job, I'm a kid."

"Sounds like your problem. Not mine."

"When Liam goes to the store with his mom, she lets him get anything he wants. Pop-Tarts, Toaster Strudel, Twix bars, Pringles, whatever."

"That's because Liam is a spoiled brat. And his mom is rich."

"They aren't rich just because they live in a house."

"Well, they're richer than us!" Mom shouts. She gets out of the car and slams the door. I don't take off my seat belt. Mom storms around the car and tries to open the door. It takes a second 'cause it has a big dent in the side that catches every time. Metal wrenches against metal when she jerks it open. "Get out of the car!"

"Can I get just one thing I want?"

"You can get an ass-whoopin' if you don't get out of the car this minute."

Not budging, I stare straight ahead. My arms cross like a shield. I don't know why I get so angry about this stuff. This is how it's been my whole life. But some days—some days I hate my life, and I feel like fighting. Fighting my mom, fighting other kids, fighting the world. Doesn't matter. Just something to take the sting out of me being so broke.

"I'm going to count to three!" Mom growls through gritted teeth. I see her fingers curl into her palms, making fists. "One—"

"Fine!" I shout back. I get out of the car and slam the broken door, the metal catching like robot nails on a chalkboard. Usually, I stand my ground. But when Mom gets that red look in her eyes, I know . . . it's better to stop arguing.

I pull a shopping cart from the pen. One of the wheels is wonky and spins left and right instead of rolling straight. I consider putting it back, getting a new one, but then I feel bad for it. It's not the cart's fault it's messed up.

We make our way down one aisle and then another. My mouth is watering. There's aisles full of food—peanut butter, pasta, stuff to make tacos or burgers, all kinds of cereal, practically a thousand kinds of chips and dips and salsas, then cookies, Chex mix, beef jerky, fried mozzarella sticks, waffles, Granny Smith apple pies, donuts, dozens of different flavors of ice cream.

And I can't get any of it.

I know better than to ask for anything. Mom's answer is always "No." Or "No way." Or "Are you crazy? Put it back. It's too expensive."

It's crazy to say a bag of potato chips is too expensive. A whole bag costs, like, four bucks. That seems like a lot of money, but it can be ten little meals. That's only like forty cents each.

Now my stomach is really growling and grumbling. I try to ignore it as I push the empty cart behind Mom. This morning, we only had enough Cheerios and milk for like half a person. I got up first, and I could have eaten it. I didn't though. I saved them for Ford. He's my baby brother, and he's only two. So he needs it more.

Mom shoves an open envelope into my hand. Inside is an overdue bill. I ask, "What's this for?"

"On the back, stupid," she says.

On the back is a grocery list. Mom's tall, loopy, cursive handwriting is hard to read, but it says all the stuff we need. Milk. Cereal. Bread. That kinda junk. My mom usually sticks to the list, but some days she changes her mind based on the yellow signs for today's specials or clearance items.

"Look! This ground beef is on sale for a dollar!" she says.

The meat is all weird brown though. I scrunch my face. "Raw beef's supposed to be pink."

Mom rolls her eyes, throwing it in the cart. "It's still good. Just cook it well done."

Turning from one aisle to the next, I see the lady with free samples. I leave the cart behind to run over. With a smile, she asks, "Would you like to try a Maplewood Sausage?"

I grab a toothpick-stabbed mini-bite, dip it in the mustard, and shove the whole thing in my mouth. I savor the juicy explosion of flavor. But it's gone too soon. Before the lady can object, I take two more. I make sure to smile and say "Thank you."

"Mom, free samples." I point. "It's so good. Can we buy some?"

Mom ignores me. Too busy digging through her folder of coupons. She spends all day Sunday, every Sunday, cutting coupons out of the newspaper. Then she makes sure we only go grocery shopping on Tuesdays. Tuesdays are *Double-Coupon Day*.

"Yes!" Mom says in victory. "This coupon is for two dollars off! Double, that means four dollars in savings!"

"Since you're saving four dollars, can we get a box of mac-n-cheese?"

"No."

"But it's Ford's favorite."

"He's a toddler, he doesn't have a favorite anything."

When we round the next corner, there's another samples person. This guy has cheese and crackers. But there's no sign that says *Free*. Trying to be polite, I ask, "Are these free?"

He gives me a dirty look. "If you're going to buy some."

"Hey!" my mom shouts. "I don't see a sign saying anything about buying nothing. Rex, go ahead. Have as many as you want."

I feel my face redden. I'm hungry, but I don't want to be rude. I take the smallest cracker with a little square of cheese on it. I whisper, "Thank you."

"Don't thank him," Mom snaps at me, glaring at him. "He thinks he's so much better than us, but he's the one selling cheese."

The cheese man mutters under his breath, "Trailer trash."

"We don't live in a trailer anymore!" Mom shouts at him. "So there!"

She takes control of the cart and pushes us away. I'm relieved. For a second, I thought she was going to pick a fight. It wouldn't be the first time. My mom doesn't shy away from much. Especially confrontation.

As we move toward the checkout, a few minutes later, Mom is still agitated, talking to herself like a crazy person. "—looking down on us. He doesn't even know me. He doesn't know my situation. Thinks he's so much better than us. Screw him."

At the register, I transfer the items from the cart onto the conveyor belt. The cashier watches me as I look at the candy racks. Cashiers always look at me like they're watching to see if I'll steal something. Like I'm guilty, 'cause my clothes are from a second-hand store.

While the cashier rings up stuff, Mom pulls out her wallet. She's counting money, except the money looks different from usual. I've never seen it before. It looks like toy money, like from that game Monopoly. It's all bright colored, and says FOOD COUPON.

"What is that?" I ask.

"Don't worry about it," Mom snaps. She pushes me toward the end of the counter. "Don't just stand there being lazy. Bag the groceries."

The cashier finishes scanning, then does the discount for the coupons. She says the total. Mom hands her the weird, fake-looking money. The cashier punches some buttons and says, "After the food stamps, you owe ten dollars and thirty-eight cents."

"What are food stamps?" I ask.

"Don't worry about it," Mom repeats, but this time, she scowls at me.

Stamps are for the post office. So I wonder if my mom is going to mail our food home. But that doesn't make any sense. We drove here, so we can drive the groceries home like normal.

Mom pours all the cash and change out of her wallet. She unwrinkles eight one-dollar bills, then counts out 97 cents, mostly in pennies. Her hands tense up, her fingers looking like talons. She says, "I'm a little short."

The cashier shrugs, but really she's all annoyed. I can see it in her face. The woman behind us, with a full cart, throws up her arms and goes, "*What* is taking so long?" The man in line next to us clears his throat. It feels like everyone is staring at us, frustrated. Mom's face is strained, a vein popping out of her forehead. Suddenly, she seems embarrassed. I feel embarrassed too.

Mom snatches the loaf of bread from the top of the brown bag. She shoves it toward the cashier. "There! Take that off. Happy?"

Shopping is always like this. But for some reason, this time is worse. Maybe 'cause of the food stamps? Mom looks ashamed. People are staring. Then, I look at our shopping list. We didn't even get halfway down. We can't afford all our groceries.

Silence hangs between Mom and me. I carry the one bag to the car and put it in the back. When I get into the front seat, Mom starts crying. I'm not sure what to say, so I don't say anything.

We sit there for a long time.

When I reach out, to put my hand on her hand, she slaps it away. "Don't touch me! This is your fault! Do you know how expensive it is to raise an ungrateful brat?!"

I feel sick to my stomach. I don't know if it's 'cause I'm angry, or sad, or just hungry. Probably it's all three.

Ministers and priests and Buddhist monks and talk-show hosts—all those people who are supposed to be real smart and wise and stuff—always say dumb things like "Money isn't everything," or "The best things in life are free." But they're wrong.

Money *is* everything.

The best things in life *aren't* free.

And don't say something stupid like "Love is free." 'Cause it's not. It costs money to take care of the people you love. When Mom isn't working, she's always upset and sad and she can't love me like a normal mom. She gets mad at every little thing. No job means no money, which means no groceries or electricity. That makes all the love go out of my mom, like air out of a balloon. And who wants an empty balloon?

When Mom's working, she's nicer. She definitely loves me more when she has money. 'Cause she can afford groceries, and pay rent on time, bills too, all that junk—she can think straight. She remembers she cares about me.

So don't tell me love is free. 'Cause I know. *Nothing* in this world is free. Every little thing costs something.

But for some reason, things cost a whole lot more when you're poor.

MIDDLE SCHOOL

'm making sure I have everything for my first day at school tomorrow. I write down a checklist, which is kinda nerdy, but I know something is missing. The list says:

- Class schedule
- Locker number
- Lock and lock combination
- Backpack
- Pens
- Notebook
- House keys

I go over the list a bunch of times. What's missing? I get in bed at ten, but I know I won't sleep if I don't figure it out. Sometimes I get an idea in my mind and can't shut it off, and it just keeps going and going until I wanna scream. That's how I feel right now.

I can't sleep, so I get up. I pace back and forth in my room, trying to remember. I have a lot of space to do that. 'Cause I don't have any furniture, just a sleeping bag on the floor. I sit down again and look at my class schedule. I'm excited about this year. Some kids don't like school, but I'd rather be there than here at home.

In middle school, you get two electives that you get to choose yourself. Mom told me to take home economics. But that sounded stupid. I already do all that stuff at home—cooking, cleaning, taking care of a baby, balancing Mom's checkbook—I don't want to do it at school too. Instead, I chose art. Like painting and drawing.

Around eleven, I finally remember what I need—lunch money.

In the living room, Mom and Sam are on the couch, cuddled up. The TV is on, but they're whispering and giggling about something else.

"Hey, Mom—"

"What are you doing up?" she snaps. "You're supposed to be asleep."

"I forgot my lunch money."

Mom nudges Sam, saying, "This kid is always 'Gimme, gimme, gimme.' Ugh." They both laugh.

"No, I'm not," I argue. "But I need lunch money. I have to eat."

"D-d-do you?" Sam stutters. He's not making fun of me, that's just how he talks. "M-my d-d-dad used to m-make m-me work f-for lunch m-money."

Mom smiles this cruel smile, saying, "Did you know, a hundred years ago, parents just kicked their kids out on the street? They had to fend for themselves. Like 'Hansel and Gretel.' Too bad it's not still like that."

"Yeah, too bad," I say. "Can you just give me my lunch money, so I can go to bed?"

"You don't need lunch money this year." Mom turns around, going back to the TV show. "You're in the Free Lunch Program."

"The what?" I ask.

Mom grunts, annoyed that she has to explain. "It's a program where poor people don't have to pay for their kids' food. Manuela's mom told me about it in the laundry room, so I enrolled you."

"What? Why can't you just pay for my lunch? We're not that poor."

Mom practically flies off the couch and grabs my arm. Squeezing so hard, her fingers dig past the muscle and into the bone. "Why don't *you* pay for your lunch? Or better yet, call your *father* and ask him to pay for it?"

"He sends a child-support check every month," I yell. "Isn't that what it's for? To feed me?"

"*You are fed!*" Mom screams, shaking me hard. "And you're clothed, you have a roof over your head, you don't have to work! That's more than a lot of people have, you spoiled little brat!"

I try to wrench myself free, but can't. So I scream back at her, "*How can I be spoiled when I live in this dump with you?*"

I shouldn't have said that. I know it the second it comes out of my mouth. But you can't unsay things. The stuff that happens next—

I don't want to talk about it.

FAMILY

My oldest memory is of my parents fighting. Not Sam. I mean Mom and my real dad. Before they got a divorce.

The three of us lived in this trailer park in San Antonio. When they fought, the entire trailer would shake. It felt like an earthquake, like the world was falling apart as the gods pounded on each other. Like their battle might rattle the universe until everything was destroyed. Then I'd be left alone in the darkness of space.

Dad left when I was five. Mom had a bunch of boyfriends after that. Each one more of a jerk than the next. Then she met Sam. He was the maintenance man for our apartment complex. At first he was all nice and taught me how to ride a bike and swim real good and took me out for pizza. Then he started hitting my mom.

I kept hoping he would go away. Then they had Ford, who was named after Sam's favorite car (which seems kinda weird to me). Having the same mom makes Ford my baby brother. He's not a baby, but he sure acts like it. He's two and a half and about the most annoying kid I've ever met. I still love him though, 'cause he's my brother so I have to. Even when he destroys my stuff.

I have to watch Ford all the time, and take care of him too. Every day, I make his food, let him watch dumb baby shows instead of my shows, and play with him and stuff. I'm trying to teach him to read, and he can, a little. He's real smart. But when he doesn't get his way, he screams bloody murder! It's so annoying. I'm glad I finally potty trained him. Now I don't have to change his diapers anymore. That was disgusting.

Still, it's not fun to spend all my free time watching him. Especially when my friends are out riding bikes and seeing movies and doing cool stuff, you know? So yeah.

Sam has been around for five years now. He says he's my stepdad, but he's not. Him and my mom aren't even married.

One time, he was real drunk, and like, half passed-out on the couch. I got all curious and asked why he stuck around, especially 'cause all him and Mom do is fight. He said, "F-f-for Ford." I guess a lot of parents do that, stick around for their kids.

My dad didn't do that though. He left me behind. No problem.

After a few years in San Marcos, Mom decided to move. Sam and her moved us around a bunch till we got here. Since getting to Birmingham, Mom and Sam fight more than usual. Sometimes it's about stupid stuff. Usually it's about money. Probably 'cause both of them can't find work.

Mom says getting a job is harder than it sounds. Which is weird, 'cause restaurants always have fliers up for dishwashers. How hard can it be to wash dishes? I do it all the time and no one pays me.

Help Wanted signs are all over town. There's even a bunch of listings in a "Jobs" section in the newspaper. I tried to help once, by going through the paper and circling a bunch of things that sounded OK. Mom got all pissed. She shouted, "I'm not doing that crap!"

Sam got all mad too, and was all like, "Th-that j-job's for Sp-spics, for y-your p-people. Me? I'm wh-wh-white. I d-deserve b-better."

Sam and Mom don't have jobs right now.

Anyway. The four of us live in a two-bedroom, one-bathroom apartment. It's nice I guess. We're on the second floor so we get sunlight. And our porch overlooks the courtyard, where kids play and stuff.

There's no real furniture in our place except an itchy tweed couch and an old black-and-white TV. Sam found both behind a dumpster when we first moved here. He made me help carry them and I almost broke my back. Mom freaked 'cause of germs, and spent, like, two days cleaning them over and over. Oh, and I guess Sam and Mom have a bed that someone gave them. Ford sleeps with them.

In my room, there's just a sleeping bag and some cardboard boxes for my clothes. I also have a bunch of books. I like reading. I used to have more stuff, but every time we moved, Mom left more of my stuff behind. Especially the presents from my dad. Lots of other kids have a ton of stuff in their rooms. And usually their parents have a lot of stuff in the rest of the house too.

Compared to them we don't have much. I don't mind though. Some of my friends get yelled at when they break stuff in their house. In my apartment, there's nothing to break.

LUNCH MONEY

As soon as I step onto the school bus, Liam Forrester shouts, "Look at that shiner! Holy crap!"

The bus driver looks in the rearview mirror at Liam and warns, "Language!"

Liam is always like this, being loud and the center of attention. He does this thing where he's smiling and laughing at the same time, so you never get real mad at him. He's just this fun, happy guy. He's been my best friend since I moved to Birmingham, Texas. He lives in Grayson Village, the really nice housing development behind Vista Nueva, the apartment complex where I live.

Before I sit in the seat he saved for me, he asks, "What'd you do to your face this time, klutz?"

"Ran into a door," I lie.

It's not just Mom's fault—it's mine too. I shouldn't have raised my voice at her. I really do try to be a good kid, but sometimes I get so angry. Everything turns red. Feels like my blood is on fire and I'm going to puke or pass out or . . . I don't know. Next thing I know, I'm screaming so hard. But that's all I do is yell.

I don't hit my mom back—not even when she's really hurting me.

"You get more black eyes than I do in Taekwondo." Liam laughs. "You should try out for the football team with me. Then at least you'll have a helmet."

The whole bus ride, I'm trying to get excited about middle school like I was all summer. But I can't. There are three elementary schools in Birmingham and only one middle school. That means there will be a bunch of new students. Everyone's going to stare at my eye and wonder what happened. I don't want anybody to know the truth. It's embarrassing. Girls are lucky they get to wear makeup. If it happened to them, they could probably just cover it up and no one would even know.

In my first three classes, history, math, and English, I can barely focus. Students keep looking at me. Two girls in the next row keep passing notes back and forth in class. One of them nods at me. Then both girls giggle.

Teachers notice too. When I walk into my new English class, Mrs. Winstead sees the holes in my shoes, my too-small jeans, my too-big shirt, my secondhand backpack, and my black eye. Right then, she decides she doesn't like me. I know 'cause she gives me this real awful look, like the cashiers in the grocery store. With the tip of her finger, she moves a strand of gray hair back into place, and adjusts her glasses. Then she announces to the class, "There will be no fighting in or outside of my classroom. I have a zero-tolerance policy for violence. Is that understood?" She says it to the classroom, but she's looking at me the whole time.

See? She thinks I'm trouble. Now I'll have to work extra hard to prove I'm not. Which sucks big-time. This isn't the way I wanted to start school.

After third period, it's lunchtime. Which is good, 'cause I'm starving. When I finally find my way to the cafeteria, there's this huge line to get food. I look for anyone I know. There's a few, but no friends I'm real tight with, so I can't cut or anything. I get in line. I've never seen so many students. Someone said there's like two thousand students who go here, though that seems like a lot. There are a lot of tables though—maybe a hundred of them. Looking for Liam is like looking for a nickel in a dumpster full of trash.

I finally see Liam at a table. He waves to come sit with him. That's a relief. At least now I know where I'm sitting after I get my food.

The line moves fast. I get my plastic tray and hold it out. The cafeteria workers remind me of my abuela, my mom's mom. She's from Mexico. So after each of the lunch ladies gives me a spoonful of mashed potatoes or green beans or fish sticks, I make sure to say "Gracias."

As I grab a carton of chocolate milk, I remember I don't have lunch money. To make it worse, I have no idea how this Free Lunch Program thing works. My stomach gets all tight and sick-feeling. I watch the three kids in front of me, hoping one of them knows how to do it so I can watch them go first. But each of them pays with cash. I look around. There's people everywhere. It's not like I can sneak off with my lunch. I wouldn't do that anyway. I'm poor, but I don't steal.

My face is hot and my forehead is sweating. So are my hands.

I hate this. Why couldn't my mom give me the money? At least for the first day of school? Why can't things ever just be easy?

"Two dollars," the cashier says.

"Oh, um . . ." I start. But I don't know what to say. I keep looking behind me, I don't know why. Probably 'cause everyone is watching.

"Sweetie, it's two dollars," she says. The cashier is old, probably about ninety. Her thin body seems so fragile she might break. She's squinting behind thick, smudged glasses.

"I'm on the . . . you know," I say.

"Hmm?"

"The Program," I say. "The thing where, you know, the uh, thing."

"You're going to have to speak up," the cashier says. "I'm deaf in one ear."

Students behind me are getting aggravated. "What's the holdup?" "Come on, man." "I'm hungry."

I lean as close to the cashier as possible, saying, "I'm in the Free Lunch Program."

"I'm sorry, dear, one more time?" she asks, pointing her ear at me.

"I'm in the Free Lunch Program!" I snap. I don't do it on purpose. Like I said, though, sometimes I get angry.

"No need to raise your voice at me," the cashier says. She pulls out a red binder and begins flipping through the tabs. "What's your name?"

I want to scream. Students behind me are restless. Everyone

is looking at me, saying, "Pay and go, dude." "Why is he taking for-*ever*?" "I wanna eat today."

"Your name?" the cashier asks again.

I try to say my name in a nice tone, but I can't help gritting my teeth. "Rex Ogle."

The old lady licks her thumb before she turns each page. She finally finds my name, and places a red check mark next to it. "There we go."

I don't thank her. I grab my tray and walk away as fast as I can.

My heart is pounding in my chest. My palms are all wet. My lungs are tight, like I can't get enough air. I never got like this at school in fifth grade. School always felt safe, an escape from home stuff. I only ever get like this when Mom is acting crazy, or Sam is starting something. I wonder if I'm sick, or having a heart attack, or if I'm going crazy. I shake my head. I'm not like my mom. I'm not crazy. I can control this.

I take a deep breath. Then another.

I finally get to Liam and realize the tables only have eight seats each. And his table is full. Before I can stop myself, I growl, "Thanks for saving me a seat."

"Chill, man. I tried, but it's the first day." Liam leans over to his other friend, Derek. "Yeesh. He's acting like my girlfriend or something." They both laugh at me.

When I storm off, I slam my shoulder into some short kid. I yell, "Get out of the way, idiot." I regret it immediately, but I don't apologize. I keep walking.

I end up sitting at an empty table on the second level. From here, I can see Liam and Derek laughing—probably about me. All around the cafeteria, people are sitting with their friends. Except me. I'm sitting alone.

This year was supposed to be great. It's only the first day, and everything is falling apart already. Yesterday, I was so excited. Now, I'm angry and pissed off and alone. All 'cause of . . . 'cause of what? I come to school with a black eye and have to beg for a free lunch. It's bull crap. No one should have to ask for handouts. No one. Especially not kids. Now everyone knows I'm nothing but trailer trash.

This was supposed to be a good year.

I guess it won't be after all.

BUTT WORMS

After school, I try to call Abuela. When I pick up the phone, there's no dial tone. Just silence.

"Mom, the phone isn't working."

"Yeah. Because I didn't pay the phone bill," Mom says. "It's a waste of money. The only people who call are bill collectors anyway."

"And Abuela!" I remind her.

Mom rolls her eyes. "If my mother wants to talk to us so bad, let her pay for our phone line."

"She offered to!"

"I don't need her money. And we don't need a phone."

"But I told her I would call her after my first day."

"Then use the pay phone by the laundry room. Call her collect. She'll love that."

I don't think Abuela loves it. Collect calls are real expensive. Like a dollar for the first minute, and fifty cents every minute after. Still, I know my grandma worries when our phone line gets cut off and she doesn't hear from us. So when I call, she accepts the charges anyway.

"Hola, Abuela," I say.

"¿Cómo está, mi nieto favorito?" she asks. I can hear her smile on the other end of the phone.

"Grandma, you know I don't speak Spanish."

She laughs. With her thick accent, she says, "I know, but you should learn. It will help you get a job."

"I'm too young for a job!"

"Is that so?" she laughs again. Her voice is always warm when I call. "Tell me about you. How is my favorite person in the whole world?!"

"I'm good," I say. I don't want to get all serious. "I miss you."

"I miss you too. I miss you more than you can possibly imagine. Or measure. Te amo."

"I love you too," I say. I love talking to her too, 'cause she's always real kind and happy, and she always tells me how much she cares for me. I know that seems like baby stuff, but sometimes it's nice to hear.

"The teachers must love you at school. You are so handsome and so smart and so polite."

"I don't know about that," I say.

"Hmm. You do not sound like you are enjoying school. Are you?"

I know she wants me to say yes, but I hate lying. "Not really."

"Are the classes difficult?"

"No."

"Are the teachers nice?"

"Some of them."

"Then what is it?"

I try to think of how to say the truth without worrying my abuela. She knows about my mom, and how she gets. But there's nothing either of us can do. So I say, "Everyone at my school is rich. They all have nice clothes and nice school supplies and their parents look really nice when they drop them off at school. Those kids have everything, and they don't even care! I wish that was my life."

"There is no such thing as wishes," Abuela says. "Do not spend your time wanting things you cannot have. Be clean and dress nice and neat. Be polite. Make good grades. You will do well. You are so, so, so brave, hijo."

"You only say that 'cause I'm your grandson," I say.

"Yes," she says with a laugh, "but also because it is true!"

But the more I think about it, the more frustrated I get. "Abuela, you don't understand how hard it is. Everything is so easy for everyone else. 'Cause they have money. Normal stuff is, like, a hundred times harder for me, 'cause I don't have money. It's not fair."

Abuela grows quiet. When she speaks, she picks her words carefully. Still warm, but also serious. Honest. "Life is not always fair."

"Well, that sucks!" I don't mean to yell but I do. Quickly, I say, "I'm sorry. I'm not mad at you, Abuela. I just want things to be easier."

"When I was your age," Abuela says, "my family and I lived in a single-room house in Mexico. It had four walls, a dirt floor, and a roof that leaked when it rained. There was no plumbing, no running water, no toilet. We had to go outside if we needed to make number one or number two, day or night, summer or winter. I lived in that tiny place with my mother, my father, and my thirteen brothers and sisters.

"Growing up, two of my sisters died because they got sick. Antibiotics could have saved their lives. But my parents did not have money for the medicine. Do you think that was fair? No. My life has not been easy. But we made it work. And you will make this work too."

"Abuela, I didn't know," I say, embarrassed. "I didn't know about your sisters. I'm so, so sorry."

"Do not be. This is life. God works in mysterious ways. He took them up to heaven so that they did not suffer anymore. The next year, my father found work. He did not make a lot of money, but when my twin brother grew sick, we had money for medicine. My brother got better. Now, he is a doctor in Mexico. A doctor! One day, you could be a doctor if you wanted to."

"I don't know what I want to be when I grow up," I say.

"You will figure it out. Until then you need to work hard. Do you understand?"

I shake my head, even though she can't see me, saying, "Yeah. But I don't have to like it, do I?"

Abuela laughs. "Do you think I like working every day? No! Of course not. But I do it. With the money I make, I send some to each of my children, to my grandchildren, and to my brothers and sisters and parents back home in Mexico. It is hard, but I do it."

"Wow, I didn't know that either," I say. "Why didn't you ever tell me?"

"I do not want to brag. But it is important you hear this. You are old enough now to know such things."

"Thank you for sharing, Abuela. You're amazing, you know that?"

"No. I am just me. And you are just you. But you are strong. Fuerte."

"It'd still be easier if we were rich," I say. "Everyone in Birmingham has money. They live in big houses and wear jewelry and all the kids get whatever they want. It's like being at the mall with no money. You see everything you want, but can't have anything. Being broke is a pain in the butt."

"Butt pain?" Abuela laughs. "When I was a little girl, my sister had parasites. Parasites are very common in Mexico. They are giant tapeworms that grow inside your intestines to eat your food and steal your nutrients. We knew my sister had them, because she was always itching down there. When we looked, sometimes you could see the tip of the worm coming out of her anus. My parents could not afford a doctor for this. But she was in pain. So one night, my mother and I helped by pulling the tapeworm out of my sister, out of her butt. It was almost two feet long. *That* was painful."

SCHOOL SUPPLIES

om is counting her food stamps as we walk into Walmart. This sinking feeling grips my stomach as I look around, hoping no one sees the food stamps, hoping there's no kids from my school watching.

"I forgot my list at home," she says, "Remind me to get milk."

"Get milk," I say, trying to be funny.

Mom shoots me a nasty glare. I know that look. It means *Don't piss me off.* So I don't say anything else until I wheel the cart into the aisle with school supplies.

I'm lucky Mom even let me come with her this time. All week, she's been complaining about buying me school supplies, saying she doesn't want to waste the gas. Luckily, Abuela sent the school-supply money. In her letter, there were two twenty-dollar bills wrapped in foil, with a card that read "Buy yourself nice things for school." Mom took one of the twenties. So now I only have twenty left.

I hate that Mom and Sam are in charge of me. Adults aren't always smarter than kids. I'm always doing stuff that parents should do. Like hooking up the wires for the TV or the stereo, or jump-starting a car. That stuff is easy for me. Mom doesn't even know how to make toast, and I can cook, like, twenty kinds of meals, even stuff without recipes. Plus, I know a bunch of facts 'cause I read a lot.

I for sure know more than Sam. He can barely write a full sentence. Sometimes he has me fill out job applications for him. And I'm good at math. Mom has me double-check hers in her checkbook all the time. She spends more money than she has. Then the bank calls and she flips out. She thinks she "bounced" a check, which doesn't make any sense. Paper doesn't bounce. So see? Mom doesn't even know easy vocab words.

Mom says, "Oops. I forgot your supply list at home."

I know this trick. She did this last year when she didn't want to buy my school supplies. I pull the list out of my own pocket. "I didn't forget. I need pencils, pens—"

"Why do you need *both*?"

I shrug. "—binders, hole-punched loose-leaf paper, notebooks—"

"Why do you need loose-leaf paper *and* notebooks?"

I shrug again. "It's what the list says."

Mom sneers. "You're *not* getting both. It's a waste of money. You can get the notebooks with the hole punched paper. Then you can pull it out if you need it."

I argue, "But it'll have the frayed edges. I can't turn in my homework like that—"

Another glare from Mom. I stop complaining. "I also need note cards, highlighters—"

"For what?"

"Studying, I guess." I'm not sure. But I like the idea of getting highlighters. I reach for a four pack, with neon pink, yellow, green, and orange.

Mom looks at the price. "*Four ninety-seven?!* Nuh-uh. No way. Put it back. You can have *one* highlighter." She grabs the cheapest version and throws it in the cart.

"The list says highlighters—*plural*, as in more than one."

"I don't care. What else?"

"A backpack—"

"You can use your backpack from last year!" she shouts.

I shout back, "I know that! I'm just reading!" Except I'm not. My backpack from last year has a giant hole in the bottom. I have to wear it upside down so nothing falls out. Mom either doesn't know or doesn't care. I'd say my money's on the second one, but I don't have money to make bets.

I continue reading from the list. "A calculator—"

"You're going to middle school, *not* a job! What do you need a calculator for?" Mom yells. She's so loud, another mom in the aisle looks at us.

"I don't know. It says I need it for pre-algebra."

"Can't you take a math class that *doesn't* need a calculator?"

"Everyone uses calculators in middle school," I say, not sure if that's even true.

Mom takes one look at the price of the cheapest option and shouts, "No way, Jose! Abuela only sent you twenty dollars—" It takes all my willpower to not point out Abuela sent forty. "I'm not paying for this crap. The school can provide it if you need it so bad. In fact, why can't the school provide everything? That's what my taxes pay for, don't they?"

"I don't know anything about taxes!"

"You should go to school and tell your principal I refuse to buy your supplies. I bet he'll have some lying around somewhere."

"I'm not doing that!" Mom always says crazy stuff like that. She means it too. That's why I'm shouting. "Just buy me the stuff I need, OK?"

Mom grabs my arm hard and shakes me. "Watch the way you talk to me."

I yank my arm back from her grip. "Or what?!"

"Is *that* how you want to play this? Fine!" she shrieks. She abandons the cart in the middle of the aisle and walks toward the exit. "I won't buy anything! Is that what you want?"

"No!"

"Apologize, then."

I cross my arms. "No."

"*Apologize!*" she screams.

A group of moms is staring at us. They're dressed real nice. At least, nicer than my mom. They have colorful clothes, combed hair, even some sparkling jewelry. They look like normal moms.

My mom doesn't look like that. She hasn't showered today, so her hair's all messy. She's wearing old sweat-bottoms, a stained shirt, and flip-flops. She doesn't wear makeup. My mom doesn't have any jewelry on. 'Cause she doesn't own any.

I push my rage down. I quiet my voice, saying, "People are staring."

"Who? *Them?!*" Mom shouts, pointing to the other moms. "I don't know them! I don't care what they think!" When my mom makes a scene in public, it makes my skin crawl. 'Cause everyone stops to watch. It's like a bus crash. People can't look away. Then everyone knows how sad and messed up my life is.

Mom hisses, "Apologize to me now, or we're walking out of this store and you can go to school with nothing."

I hesitate. I want to shout back. I want one of the other moms to defend me. I want my mom to get arrested or go away and one of the nice moms to adopt me. But that's not going to happen. Finally, I cave. I whisper, "I'm sorry."

"I can't hear you," Mom yells.

"I said, I'm sorry!" I yell back.

Mom smiles, victorious. "Was that so hard?"

I don't know how she does it. My mom doesn't care what other people think about her at all. She wheels past the gawking and horrified mothers, her head held high and proud, saying, "What are *you* looking at?"

As I pass the offended crowd, I lower my head.

Money seems like such a dumb, weird thing. Coins and pieces of paper and checkbooks and numbers in bank accounts. Really, it's just invisible digits floating around. Still, I wish I had it.

If I had money, I wouldn't have to fight with my mom in a grocery store about school supplies. If I had money, I could pay my parents' bills, so we could live in a nice house like other people. If I had money, I could dress nice, like the kids I go to school with. If I had money, I'd share it with people who don't, so they wouldn't have to feel the way I do now.

If I had money, I'd be happy.

But I don't. And I'm not.

TARDY

t's raining cats and dogs this morning. I don't have an umbrella. By the time I get to the school bus, I'm soaked through. At first I think it's kinda funny. I squish under my arms and make fart noises and everyone on the bus laughs.

An hour later, at school, I'm still wet. My shoes squeak loud when I walk, and my fingers are all wrinkled. My first class, the room is freezing, like how I imagine the North Pole in the dead of winter, Santa's elves hiding for cover. The giant Texas-sized air conditioners hum loud, but I can barely hear anything over the chattering of my teeth. Shivering so hard I think my goose bumps are gonna stay there forever. Finally the bell rings and I run to the bathroom. My lips are blue in the mirror so I take off my clothes and run them under the heated hand dryer. Every time someone comes in, they look at me like I'm crazy.

When I get to third period, Mrs. Winstead says, "You're tardy."

"What's that mean?" I ask.

Everyone laughs at me. Turns out *tardy* is some dumb, fancy way of saying *late*. I don't know why she couldn't just say that.

At least it's Friday. It's been a sucky first week.

I've barely seen my friends from last year. Todd and Zach have different schedules. So does Liam, but he saves me a seat at the lunch table when he can. In fifth grade, the four of us had Mrs. Kingston. We goofed off every day together. During and after school. Now we don't have any of the same classes.

"Ogle!" I turn around and it's Zach. We bump fists. I was just thinking about him, but I don't say that. Don't want to sound, you know, gay or something. He says, "I haven't seen you all week. Where've you been hiding?"

"Nowhere. This school is gi-normous. There's so many students."

"Tell me about it. Hey, you heading to lunch? Let's sit together."

I'm excited to sit with Zach. I hope we can find Liam and Todd. We can sit together, like old times. Then I remember the whole Free Lunch thing.

Zach is hilarious, but he makes fun of people for just about anything. Last year, he found out I still played with action figures and he never let it go. He still brings it up. If he finds out about my being in the Free Lunch Program, I'll never hear the end of it. Maybe if I go after he pays, and he doesn't wait for me—

"Ladies first," he says as we get in the lunch line.

I start sweating. I say, "Then *you* should go first."

"No way," Zach says. "You're more girly than me."

"No, I'm not!" I snap. More defensive than I mean to be.

Zach copies me, but in a high-pitched girl voice. "No, I'm not!"

The two seventh graders behind us laugh. I can feel my face burning red. I hate this. I'm not even hungry now. I feel sick. If

I stay, Zach will make fun of me. If I leave, he'll make fun of me. So I stay. I stand up a little straighter and push my chin out, the way Zach stands.

He notices and says, "Don't copy me, weirdo."

"I'm not," I sneer. I pick up the plastic lunch tray and go through the line. I nod to the lunch lady. "I'll take the chicken nuggets."

"I'll take the chicken nuggets," Zach repeats in his high girl voice. Last summer, I would've thought that was funny. But not now. Everything feels like it sucks these days.

When I'm about to pay, I say: "I forgot my silverware. I have to go back and get it. Why don't you pay, and go find us a table, I'll catch up."

"OK, stupid," Zach says.

I take my time picking out a fork, watching as Zach pays the cashier and leaves. Then, I get back in line.

"Two dollars," the cashier says.

I try hard not to roll my eyes or growl or snap. Every day, the cashier and I have the exact same conversation. Why can't she just remember? "Free Lunch Program," I say as quickly and quietly as possible. The two seventh graders behind me are talking, but I'm pretty sure they exchange a glance.

"Name?" the cashier asks.

"Rex Ogle."

She adds the checkmark.

Walking to catch up with Zach, I finally catch my breath again. I wonder if I'll have to go through this every single time I want to have lunch with a friend.

FOOTBALL

———

When the bell rings, the school hallways get crazy. It's like a big river of kids rushing around, but like the dangerous-rapids kind in the movies. There's only four minutes between classes. You leave one class, grab books from your locker, and head to the next class. Four minutes isn't long. It's barely enough time for me to figure out my locker combo.

Birmingham Middle has sixth, seventh, *and* eighth graders. So everyone's bigger than me. I've always been kinda short and scrawny for my age. Since my birthday's in August, I'm also younger than most kids in my class. It sucks, 'cause I walk out, and it's like BAM! I get hit by these eighth-grade giants who aren't watching where they're going. And then WHAM! I get slammed by someone's backpack. Then SMASH! I crash right into a locker. It's like a pinball machine, and I'm the little silver ball that everyone is whacking and slapping around.

By lunchtime, I feel like a dead punching bag. But today, I finally have some luck. Liam, Todd, Zach, and I are finally able to sit together. Liam's friend Derek is there too though. I'm pretty sure he hates me. I don't know why. He always disagrees with me, and looks at me like I'm hiding something. Three guys I don't know take the other seats.

"It's only the third week of school, but I can already tell you, I hate Mrs. Constance. Who needs science anyway?" Zach says.

"She's the worst," Todd agrees.

"Totally," Liam adds.

"All of you are in the same class?" I ask.

"Yeah, we have a few classes together," Todd says. "Why aren't you in any with us?"

'Cause God hates me, I want to say. Instead, I shrug. "I don't know."

"In the remedial classes with the retards?" Zach laughs.

"No." I start to reach into my backpack to prove it with my schedule.

Zach adds, "Or are you one of those homos in all honors classes?" Todd and Liam laugh. I leave my schedule in my backpack. I'm in three honors classes. But I don't want anyone to think I'm a homo.

"Who's trying out for football?" Derek asks.

Liam, Todd, and Zach raise their hands. Then I do too, saying, "Awesome!" We all high-five.

"*You're* trying out?" Derek asks me.

"Why wouldn't I?"

"You're too small. You'll get crushed."

I feel anger rising in my throat. Derek's always looking for a way to put me down. But Liam says, "What are you talking about? He could be a safety, or a punt returner, or a running back. Being smaller works for those positions."

"See?" I say, even though I don't know what those positions are. I've never played football. I don't even watch it, 'cause our TV sucks. It barely gets two channels. But if I can teach myself all the stuff I've already taught myself, I can learn football easy.

"I've seen you in gym class," Derek says. "You'll still get crushed."

Liam laughs. "You realize you're like half an inch shorter than Ogle, right?"

"No, I'm not!" Derek turns red in the face. Todd and Zach start cracking up. I do too. Seeing Derek all angry makes me really happy. He's such a jerk. I decide I'm going to join the football team just to piss him off.

———

IT TAKES ME ALMOST A WEEK TO GET UP THE COURAGE TO ASK Mom and Sam. If I want to be on the football team, I need a parent's signature. I'm going to ask tonight.

Sam says cooking is women's work. But Mom doesn't know how to cook. So in our house, I make the meals. Today was Double-Coupon Day, so we actually have food in the house. I make Hamburger Helper for dinner. I set the table with paper plates, folded paper towels, plastic cups, and metal utensils. Mom helps Ford into his booster seat, while I spoon the steaming meat and pasta onto the plates. Moisture forms all around the edges of the plate, where the meat heats the surface. I add a lot of salt and pepper.

Sam points at me and says, "Pull my finger."

"No," I say.

"Just do it."

When I pull his finger, he farts. Ford laughs so hard he almost chokes on his food, and Mom gets mad.

As I chew, I'm nervous to ask about football. I don't know why. Guess 'cause almost every time I ask for something, they say no. Then Mom brings it up for weeks and weeks after, saying how selfish I am. I take a deep breath, but keep eating. I wait until Mom stops grilling Sam about finding work. Then I pull the football waiver from my pocket and slide it into the center of the table. "I want to join the football team."

"Foo-baaall!" Ford says. He throws a handful of pasta. It hits me in the face.

"Th-th-that's my b-b-boy," Sam stutters. "G-g-good throw."

"Absolutely not," Mom says. "You'll get hurt."

"It can't be that dangerous. All my friends are doing it."

"If all your friends jumped off a cliff, would you do that too?" Mom always asks stupid things like that.

I say, "If it was a fun cliff."

"The answer is a big fat *no*." Mom—and I—expect the conversation to be over. But it isn't.

"N-n-now, h-h-hold on, Luciana," Sam says. "If Rex is s-s-serious, I s-s-support him. B-b-better than reading b-b-books all the time. He'd get s-s-some muscles, and maybe a g-g-girlfriend, and st-stop being s-such a s-sissy all the time."

Despite the dig, this surprises me. Sam never stands up for me.

It takes me a full minute to finally register he's on my side. "Yeah. What he said."

"No!" Mom fires back. "I am *not* signing any waivers. Rex could break his neck over some pointless game."

"It's n-n-not pointless," Sam says. "It'll h-h-help the b-b-boy make fr-friends."

"I SAID NO!" she shouts, slapping her hands on the table.

"Why not?!" I shout back. "You never let me do anything. Let me have this one thing. Please!" My black eye is finally gone, but I prepare myself for a fresh one when I see Mom's glare.

"Ju-ju-just let him tr-try out," Sam says.

"Please, Mom, I'll do whatever you want. I'll make good grades, clean the house, and—"

"I said no," she hisses. "Who cares about sports anyway?!"

"I-I d-d-do," Sam says.

"Oh, you mean, back when you were a wrestler? And how did that work out? I don't see you making any money off it now."

"W-w-watch y-your m-m-mouth, w-woman."

"Or what?! Don't threaten me!!" Mom screams. "Fine! Let him play! Who's going to pay for it? Huh? Who's paying for the helmets and the pads and the uniforms? Huh? Who's going to drive him to games? Who's going to watch Ford when we have to work and Rex is playing football? A babysitter? And who will pay for that? And what if Rex gets hurt? Huh? *Huh?!* We don't have jobs, let alone insurance. Who's going to pay for the hospital bills when he breaks his goddamn neck and I'm left wiping his ass?!"

"You won't have to wipe my ass," I say, trying to calm the situation down. But it's too late. Sam and Mom are heated.

"So who's going to pay for all of it?!" she screams. "Answer me that!"

"I-I-I'll p-p-pay for it," Sam says.

I'm not sure who's more shocked, Mom or me.

Then Mom's stare turns ice-cold. Her mouth twists into this cruel smile. "How are *you* going to pay for it, huh? You're a loser and a deadbeat. A has-been. You don't have any money. You don't even have a job."

Sam throws the whole table to the side. I barely dodge out of the way in time. Paper plates and silverware fly through the air, Hamburger Helper splatters the white walls. I've never seen the table on its side before. It feels all wrong, like gravity has reversed, or I'm in a dream.

Everything happens so fast after that. Sam is in Mom's face. Screaming, his stutter gone. Mom doesn't back down though. She's unafraid. Thrives on this. Now she gets in his face. Pointing, poking his face, his chest. Mom is screaming so hard, spit comes out. About his ice-cold mother, about his alcoholic father, about what a loser he is, how she needs to go out and find a *real* man, one that can pay the bills.

My mom knows exactly what to say to hurt someone.

When I see Ford, tears streaming down his face, his crying lost in the storm of Sam and Mom's screams—I snap back to myself. This isn't a dream.

I pick up my brother and carry him into my room. I close the door, just in time, so we don't have to see what comes next. Even behind the thin, plastic door, we can still hear it, feel it. Hear the brawl, the screams turning into thuds and gasps for air. Feel the floor vibrations of wrestling and kicking, someone trying to hold their ground, and failing. Feel two bodies crash to the floor, and hear a woman's voice wail in pain. And even though it's so quiet, even twenty feet away, I know the sound of air moving aside as a fist comes down, again and again.

I turn on the radio to block the noise. I build a pillow fort for Ford. I don't have big fancy pillows or plush couch cushions, just the one old pillow I sleep with. But I have cardboard boxes from our last move. I have thumbtacks to pin my sheets to the walls, creating new walls, and alleys and roofs, so we're hidden away in a labyrinth. I pretend out loud that I've built him a majestic castle, describing every brick and barrier and weapon that will protect him from the monsters outside.

Inside the blankets and constructed walls, hidden deep inside my sleeping bag, I turn on a flashlight and hold Ford close. I tell him made-up stories of worlds far away from here until finally he falls asleep. When I try to go to sleep, I still hear the battle outside the castle walls. I try not to move, not to cry, so I don't wake up my brother.

I'm not upset for me. I'm upset for Ford. And for my mom. Usually the fights aren't my fault. This time, it is.

―――

IN THE MORNING, FURNITURE IS OVERTURNED. A CHAIR IS MISSING a leg and a lamp is broken. Last night's dinner is still splashed everywhere, but it's all dried and crusted. A huge crater now lives in the wall, like an abstract painting. The crater is the same size as my mom's body.

And my football waiver is torn into a hundred pieces, scattered all over the living room like confetti.

When Mom comes out to make her coffee, she doesn't say a single word. She glares at me the way Derek glares at me. Like I'm filth. Dirty and disgusting. Like I'm wrong, and pathetic. Like I'm in the way. Unwelcome. The way someone looks at dog poop on the bottom of their shoe.

I want to hate my mom for hating me. I want to scream, tell her I'm joining football whether she likes it or not. I want to tell her to grow up and act like an adult and get a job and stop making my life so hard. I want to say all those things and more. But I don't.

Instead, I try to hug her.

She shoves me away. Then glares at me through a red swollen cheek and her own puffy black eye. With a busted lip, she asks, "Are you happy now?"

FREE READING

"I hate school," Liam says. We're walking from the bus to our lockers. "So stupid that we have to come."

"Yeah, I hate it too," I lie.

"I'd rather be at home," Liam says.

I don't say anything. I never want to be at home. Aside from Ford, there's nothing good there. I'd rather be at school. Here, I don't think about all the bad stuff with Mom and Sam.

When I think about that, my head gets all full up of these bad thoughts. Things I don't wanna think about. When I do, my lungs hurt, like I can't catch my breath; my stomach hurts, I feel like I want to cry. But if I start crying, I'll never stop.

Boys shouldn't cry anyway. Only girls cry.

That's why I like school. It's safe. At school, I don't think about home. I think about classes and friends or whatever. I think about art class and skateboarding and what movies everyone is talking about. I think about making good grades or being cool or popular, even though I'm not. I think about ways to keep my secret, so no one knows how stupid-poor I am. Or I just think dumb stuff like how the lock on my locker works.

I used to mess up the combo every time. It'd take me four or five tries. Now I usually get it the first time. Or the second. It's like my brain keeps forgetting if I should spin left first, or right.

Aside from the Free Lunch stuff, and Derek, who I can't stand, school is pretty good. It only took me a month, but now I know where all my classes are. Now I don't even have to look at my schedule 'cause I know it by heart.

First period is history, with Mrs. Zimmerman.

Second period is math with Mrs. Tucker.

Third period is English with Mrs. Winstead—who hates me.

Then, lunch. Which would be fun, if not for the Free Lunch Program.

Fourth period is industrial shop. Mr. Lopez is the teacher.

Fifth is computer science—which isn't science at all. We just type stuff over and over. When Mrs. Reagan isn't looking, I play games instead.

Sixth period is (actual) science with Mr. Chang.

Seventh period is art with Mrs. McCallister. She's real cool. Art is definitely my favorite class. Mrs. McCallister gives us a pizza party on the last Friday of every month just 'cause. If I was a teacher, I'd be like that. Doing nice things, just 'cause I could.

Mrs. Winstead is the opposite. She's the worst, mean to me for no reason. Well, I guess she has a reason. She's mad at me for being poor. Which isn't even my fault. You might think I'm making that up, but I'm not.

Just now, I walk into English class, she gives me this look. Like I'm gonna rob her. She clutches her purse to her chest, then puts it in her desk drawer and locks it with a key. The whole time, she watches me. I think that's pretty messed up.

It's 'cause of the way I look. My dad is white, and my mom is Mexican. I have his nose, but her skin. I tan real easy. Since I'm always outside in the Texas sun, my skin is real dark. I look full Mexican. Then there's my clothes. They're all too big for me. Mrs. Winstead probably thinks I stole them. But I didn't.

Mom buys at secondhand places, like Goodwill and Salvation Army. Or if neighbors throw out stuff, they let my mom go through the bags first. That's why a lot of my clothes are too big for me, 'cause they belonged to someone else first. Usually adults. They're not dirty though. Mom always washes them twice before I wear them.

In English class, the first thing students do is pull out notebooks. On the board are ten vocab words and ten spelling words. We're supposed to write them down. No talking. Mrs. Winstead likes it quiet.

I'm doing that, and Mrs. Winstead walks past my desk and sniffs. She *sniffs*! Like a dog smelling me.

I don't stink though. Like I said, my clothes are clean. And I shower every morning. With soap and shampoo.

Mrs. Winstead sniffs at me again anyway. Fine. Let her sniff.

After we write our words, we have "free reading" for ten minutes. Free reading means we can read whatever we want. I love reading, but not the cheesy kid stuff. I like adult stories, especially sci-fi and horror. I pull my book out of my backpack and dig in, excited. Free reading is the best part of my day, even if it is only ten minutes.

The room is silent until Mrs. Winstead snatches the book out of my hand. "What is this?"

Everyone looks at me. I don't know why she asks. I mean, she knows how to read so I'm sure she can read the title for herself. She's staring at the book cover like it's a dirty magazine.

"What is this?!" she asks again. Maybe she can't read. That'd be funny for an English teacher.

I point to the title on the book and read out loud, "Stephen King. *The Stand.*"

"You're not reading this," she says.

"I was until you took it."

"It's over a thousand pages long."

"So? It's about the end of the world. I like that kinda stuff—"

"You shouldn't lie to impress people," Mrs. Winstead says. A few of the kids snort, like they think it's funny.

"I'm not lying," I say. My face gets hot. I don't like when people stare at me. It reminds me of Mom starting fights in public. "I *am* reading it."

"In that case, you shouldn't be reading such *filth.*" Mrs. Winstead makes this face like she bit a lemon. Then her lips curl up at the ends, like she's real sly. "Perhaps I should call your mother and tell her what you're reading."

I almost say, "Go ahead." 'Cause I know our phone line got cut off. But I don't want Mrs. Winstead knowing that. Instead, I say, "My mom doesn't care. She's the one who bought it for me."

The whole class laughs. Mrs. Winstead is real mad now. She slaps the book down on my desk and storms off.

Technically, Mom didn't buy it for me. I bought it. But she knows I have it. Mom won't let me buy new books, says it's a waste of money. There's this store on Main Street though, all they have is used books. They even have a trade-in policy, so I go there a lot.

Mom's only rule about books is no sex stuff, and no romance novels, which is fine. All those covers have women falling over bare-chested men. I wouldn't be caught dead with one of those books.

But if a cover has spaceships or strange cities or monsters on it, I get all excited. I love fantasy stories. They can't happen in the real world, but I wish they could. Mainly 'cause in real life, things aren't that great. But in books, the villains—like Mrs. Winstead—are always punished. Plus there's usually a happy ending.

I like happy endings—even if they are only fantasies.

TABLES

n line for lunch, there's two girls right in front of me. Both have big blond hair and clothes that look brand-new. Both wear jewelry, gold and diamonds, even perfume. One girl says, "—Kelly's dad lost his job, and her mom's never worked, so now they're, like, totally broke. She can't even afford lunch now, so her mom makes her this pathetic bologna sandwich every day."

"*Ew*, bologna is disgusting," says the second girl.

"I know. It's so pathetic. She *cannot* sit with us at lunch anymore."

I want to tell her she's not so special, she was just born in the right family. I have this flash in my mind, of grabbing her by the hair or kicking her. Doing to her what Sam does to Mom. I don't though. I'm not like that. I would never hit a girl. Never. This big weight sits on my chest for even thinking it. I wonder if I'm evil. I can't help it though. I can't control my own thoughts sometimes.

The two girls start laughing about their ex-friend. They're awful. But there's still part of me that wants to be them. Really, I just want their money. If I had it, I wouldn't treat poor people bad. I don't get why folks act like being poor is a disease, like it's wrong or something. It's hard to be poor. Being rich is easy.

The two girls don't even look at the cashier when they hand her their cash for lunch. I bet these two don't even think about money or where it comes from. Their parents probably give them twenty bucks a day and don't blink. Meanwhile, I'm in line every day, sick to my stomach approaching the cashier. I hate it.

I've tried out all sorts of different ways to get away with my being in the Free Lunch Program. None of them have worked. Like one time, I wrote down my name and "Free Lunch Program" on paper. I handed it to the cashier, hoping she would read it, and no one around me would hear. But she said, "Oh, honey. I forgot my glasses at home. Can you read it to me?" So that didn't work.

Last week, I tried to wait to be the last student in line. No matter how many times, I said, "You can go ahead of me," there were more students. I ended up with only two minutes to eat my food before the bell rang.

Today, I have a new idea. When I get to the register, I point to the red folder and say, "Page 14. Rex Ogle." The cashier nods. Even though she's slow 'cause she's old, it's still faster than most days. She gets the red folder, finds the page, and puts the check next to my name.

It takes a second to realize it worked. I did it. I feel awesome. I didn't have to say it—those words I hate, the ones that make me feel like a beggar: *free lunch*.

My joy lasts maybe two seconds. As I walk away, the students behind me ask, "What's in the red folder?"

I don't look back. Instead, I duck my head and run until Mr. Lopez shouts, "No running in the cafeteria, Ogle!"

As if that's not bad enough, when I get to Liam's table, it's full again. "Next time come earlier," he says. Derek gives me this mean smirk.

Todd and Zach are sitting at the next table. There's only one seat left. This other kid starts to go for it, but I run over and grab it first. "Sorry."

"Dude, can you believe how sick the uniforms are?" Todd says.

"The jerseys are tight," Zach says.

"What jerseys?" I ask.

"Our football uniforms."

Liam trades seats so he can join us. "I'm so stoked we all made the team. It's gonna be so much fun."

"I know. I can't wait until our first game," Todd says. "All those cheerleaders are going to be cheering for us."

"They'll probably let us get to second base." Zach grins, making a breast-groping motion with his hands. "I hear cheerleaders are easy for football players."

"What happened to you, Ogle?" Liam asks. "I thought you were going to play too."

A sick feeling grips my stomach and twists. I think of Mom's black eye, the hole in our wall. I flick two tater tots into my mouth, motioning that I can't speak while I'm chewing. I don't know what to say. The truth isn't an option. Finally, I answer, "Football isn't really my thing."

"See, I told you," Zach says to Todd.

"Told him what?"

"That you'd pussy out. You always do."

"No, I don't," I argue.

"You do. Like that time at the skate park. You wouldn't drop in on the ramp."

"I twisted my ankle," I say.

"Whatever," Zach says, rolling his eyes.

My friends snicker. I hate being laughed at. So I say something I shouldn't. "At least I don't wear makeup to cover up my zits."

Todd and Liam burst into laughter, pointing. Zach made me promise to never tell anyone. And I never break my promises. Usually.

Why'd he have to make fun of me like that? Zach is pissed, red in the face, squeezing his hands into fists, like he's gonna hit me. If he did, I wouldn't blame him. I feel my whole body tense, the way I do before Mom or Sam hit me.

But Zach doesn't do it. Instead he says, "Screw you, fence-hopper. Go back across the border."

Now Liam and Todd are laughing at me.

"Nice one, Cover Girl," I say.

"Dirty Spic," Zach spits.

Laughing so hard they can't breathe, Liam and Todd turn strawberry red. I try to laugh too, like I think it's funny. To fit in, I guess. But it's weird laughing at myself, at the bad word I know people call my abuela. She's told me stories. So laughing at that word feels wrong.

Zach knows he's won though, so he relaxes, smiling. I wonder if all friends are this mean to one another.

The next day, when I go to sit with the guys, they're sitting at a different table. There's an open spot between Todd and Liam. When I go to sit down, Derek says, "You can't sit here. Football players only."

"Whatever." I go to sit anyways.

Derek stands up, and says, "I'm serious. You *can't* sit here."

I turn to Liam, Todd, and Zach, thinking my friends will back me up, say it's cool. Liam looks at his shoes. Todd opens his book and starts turning pages. Zach fist-bumps Derek, saying, "What he said."

Having a place to sit in middle school is important. 'Cause it means you have friends. Popular kids sit at one table. Football players sit nearby. Cheerleaders too. Band kids are in one area, school newspaper and yearbook kids at another. Religious kids have a table. So do the kids who play Dungeons & Dragons. The whole cafeteria is that way.

Everyone has their place. Everyone except me.

WHITE RABBIT

"How's middle school?" Benny asks. He's my neighbor at Vista Nueva. He has dirty orange hair and freckles covering his whole body. He's two grades under me, but we both like G.I. Joe and heavy metal music, so we hang out once in a while.

"Stupid," I say, stabbing a stick into the dirt.

"I hate school too," Benny says. He uses his dad's lighter to burn the hand off his G.I. Joe. "They put me in a dummies class because I can't read good."

"That sucks." I don't tell Benny about my grades. It's not 'cause I'm smart or anything. I'm not. I just work real hard. I'm always studying. People who are actually smart don't have to. They see or hear something, and they know it forever. My brain's not like that. Probably 'cause I'm always missing meals.

"Why do you hate school?" Benny asks.

I shrug. It's not school I hate. It's my friends. Or, the fact that I don't have any. But I don't say that.

"What are you doing, babies?" Brad asks.

"We're not babies," Benny yells at his older brother. Brad is thirteen and smokes cigarettes. He wears a leather jacket no matter how hot it is. He hangs around with Javi, the maintenance man's nephew.

"Look like babies to me." Brad takes a drag from his cigarette and blows it in Benny's face. "Playing with dolls."

"They're not dolls," Benny says. I slip my Storm Shadow and Snake Eyes figures into my pocket.

"Want to see something rated X?" Javi asks us. "Come on."

Mom told me not to hang out with Brad and Javi. She calls them a "bad influence." I don't care. She shoulda thought about that before she kicked me out of the apartment on a hot Sunday afternoon. "You shouldn't be reading when the sun is out," she said, pushing me out the front door. I told her it was homework, which it was, but she didn't care. She only gave me the boot so her and Sam could have the place to themselves while Ford naps. She's always doing that kinda stuff.

Me and Benny follow Brad and Javi. Javi takes us to his uncle's apartment. Inside, the air is cool but it smells of stale beer and cigarettes. I see a couple of cockroaches scurrying for cover. The place is littered with empty bottles, pizza boxes, dirty laundry, and old magazines. You can barely see the carpet. For once, I'm glad Mom is always cleaning our place.

"Come on." Javi leads the way into his uncle's bedroom. It's even messier than the living room. The water bed is piled with unfolded clothes. Tools and loose change are scattered everywhere on the floor. Nails, nickels, screws, dimes, pennies, washers, quarters. I wonder how much money is lying around here.

"You ready? Check this out."

Javi pulls a blanket off an aquarium. It's the biggest tank I've ever seen. Inside is a long tree branch and some rocks. It takes me a second to spot the giant snake draped over the wood.

"It's a boa constrictor," Javi says. "They can grow up to twenty feet and swallow a man whole."

"Yeah, right," Benny says.

"It's true," Brad hisses. "His uncle bought it illegally in South America. He snuck it back to the States when it was a baby. You know what it eats?" Brad grabs his little brother and presses his face to the glass. "Little girls like you!"

Benny screams. Javi and Brad laugh, even after they let Benny go. Brad is usually OK, but he always shows off in front of his friends. I hate when people show off. Even though I do it too.

"You're so stupid, Brad. I hate you!" Benny says. "I'm telling Dad!"

"Don't be like that," Brad says. "Look, I really did bring you here to show you something cool."

Javi pulls a white cardboard box from the closet. Inside is a white rabbit. "This is what the snake really eats."

My voice squeaks when I say, "Wait—what?"

"Snakes don't eat dog food. They need something alive," Javi explains. "Twice a month, my uncle gets a rabbit from the pet store. They gave this one to him for free 'cause it's blind." He waves his hand in front of the rabbit's eyes, with no reaction.

"Don't do it," Benny mumbles, his eyes welling up.

"This is nature, man," Brad says. "Big animals eat little animals."

Javi opens the aquarium, lowering the rabbit inside. The rabbit plops onto the rocks and starts sniffing around. Its little nose twitches as it stumbles. Benny tries his best not to sniffle, but he can't hide the tears.

I don't want to see it either, but I can't look away. I'm kinda both scared and excited. Reminds me of when I was eight, watching my cat have kittens. So gross, but sorta awesome too. This feels like that. And Brad is right. It is nature. When we have KFC for dinner, I eat the fried chicken right off the bones. Chickens are alive before you eat them, right? But you have to eat to live.

I wonder how hungry I'd have to be to eat a rabbit.

The four of us sit there for almost two hours, waiting to watch nature take its course. But the snake won't do it. Finally, Javi's uncle comes home.

"What are y'all doing in my room?!" he snaps.

"We wanted to watch the snake eat," Javi says. "But he won't. That blind rabbit's been in there for hours."

"This's happened before," his uncle snorts, annoyed. "Damn snake won't eat the handicapped. Senses something's wrong with it."

"Good!" Benny says. "All of you are murderers!"

"Get outta my house!" the maintenance man shouts. All four of us run out.

THAT NIGHT, I'M LYING IN MY SLEEPING BAG THINKING ABOUT the rabbit and the snake. I wonder which I am. I decide I'm the snake, 'cause snakes are pretty awesome. Plus, I want to be the eater, not the one getting eaten.

But the more I think about it, the more I think I'm wrong. At home, I'm a rabbit. Most kids are, since parents are in charge. But at school, I'm a rabbit too. Since I'm not in football, and can't pay for my own lunch, and don't have any friends. Then I began to wonder if I'm a regular rabbit or a blind one.

I start getting really upset and my stomach starts hurting so I try not to think about it. Then it's all I can think about. Stupid brain.

FAST FOOD

M om says it's cheaper, and less mess to clean, to eat fast food. We go to McDonald's the most. I don't like that they put chopped onions on their burgers, but I like the Happy Meals 'cause they come with toys. Even though I'm too old for that, it reminds me of when I was younger. Happier.

Sometimes, we go to Burger King or Jack in the Box or Taco Bell. Taco Bell is my favorite. I like the crispy tacos the best, but I only get them with meat and cheese. I hate lettuce and tomato. Then I put a bunch of hot sauce on it.

KFC is good too. But Mom says the bones in the chicken take up too much space and you don't get enough meat for your money. I also really like Wendy's 'cause they put bacon on the burger on the dollar menu, and sometimes Mom lets me get a Frosty if she has a coupon.

My all-time favorite though is Chick-fil-A. They're only in malls, and they're always closed on Sunday 'cause they're at church. Mom never lets me get it, says it's way too much money. But there's almost always a nice lady out front with free samples. I usually get one, then ask for another for my brother. But I eat it too. The chicken nuggets are amazing. When I visit Abuela in Abilene, or she comes here, we go to the mall just for Chick-fil-A. The nuggets come in this little white-and-red cardboard box. No one else does that. If it wasn't so greasy I would keep the box and put stuff in it.

"Why are you picking at your food?!" Mom snaps at me. "Aren't you hungry?"

"It's the fourth time this week we've had McDonald's," I say.

"And?"

"I don't know. It's making my stomach upset." Lately, my stomach's been hurting really bad. Like someone stabbing me with a knife. I keep telling my mom, but she won't take me to the doctor 'cause we don't have insurance.

"Most kids would love to eat McDonald's every night!" Mom shrieks.

Ford slaps his hands together, laughing, "Mah-Donooooooh's!"

"See?" Mom says. "I rest my case."

"I don't feel well," I say.

"You think it's the food?"

"I don't know," I say. "I read this article at school about how too much fast food is bad for you."

"Oh, here we go. You read one article and now you're Mr. Science! Are you a doctor now? No! You're not! Quit being a hypochondriac."

"I'm not!" I say, even though I don't know what that is. "But think about it. The food is cheap, right? That means the owners can't spend lots of money on good, fresh ingredients. What if we're not even eating real meat?"

"You're being ridiculous. It's fine. It meets all the food require-
ments. The burger has bread, meat, and cheese. And you get
veggies from the fries."

"That doesn't seem right," I say.

"What do you know? Nothing!" Mom snaps. "I've said it
before, and I'll say it again—when *you* start paying for the food,
you can choose where we eat."

THE NEXT NIGHT, MOM TAKES ME AND FORD BACK TO MCDON-
ald's, like she needs to prove a point. I ask, "Why are we back here
again?"

"I don't get you. Most kids would kill to eat burgers and fries
every night."

"Well, I'm not most kids."

"That's for damn sure!" Mom moans.

At the cashier, Mom orders for me and Ford. She always does
that. We don't get a choice. She never orders my burger plain, and
I have to pick off those little onions every time. By the time I get
off the onions, the burger is cold. The bread still tastes like onions
too. So gross.

"Will you order mine plain?" I ask. "Please?"

"Don't be difficult," Mom snaps. "Go find a seat."

I find a table close by, so I can shout "Plain!" when she orders
my burger. This time, I notice something weird. When the cashier
gives the total for our meal, Mom doesn't pull out cash or her
checkbook. She pays with some kind of coupon or voucher.

"What was that? What did you pay with?" I ask when she sits down.

Mom rolls her eyes, saying, "Mind your own business."

———

A FEW WEEKS LATER, WE'RE AT THE APARTMENT LAUNDROMAT. I'm moving clothes from the washer to the dryer. Mom is using some of the quarters to make a phone call. I pretend not to listen, but I do.

"I'm calling to report a complaint," Mom says. "The cashier at your store was very rude to me. My son ordered a burger, plain, no cheese. You see, he's allergic."

"What?" I say. "No, I'm not."

Mom slaps my arm, mouthing the words *Shut! Up!*

"That's right, lactose intolerant," Mom continues. "Terrible disease. Anyway, the burger he got had cheese. When I returned it to the cashier and explained, I asked her nicely to fix the mistake. Do you know what she did? She screamed at me!"

My mother is lying. I am not allergic to cheese. And no cashier yelled at my mom. If they had, she would have screamed back.

"Yes, ma'am. I was shocked too. I frequent your establishment at least twice a week with my whole family. I can't imagine why the cashier was so rude to me. But I thought you should know. It really ruined my experience and I just don't know if I could possibly go back—oh? You can? Well, I don't know. It really was horrible. I may tell some of my friends at church. You will? That would be wonderful. Yes. Yes. Here's my address. . . ."

———

MOM AND SAM SAY I HAVE TO EARN MY KEEP. THAT'S WHY I COOK
and clean and vacuum and take care of Ford and do laundry and
take out the trash and check the mail. We only have one mail key.
So it's on my key ring. It's my job to check the mail every day. If
I don't, I get in trouble.

I guess I'm nosy, 'cause I look at all of the mail. Every letter. It's
dumb, but I keep hoping I'll get one saying I've won the lottery. It
never happens though. No one even sends me letters. Well, except
Abuela. But today, among the overdue bills and something from
the IRS, two envelopes stand out.

One from McDonald's. The second from Taco Bell. I've seen
these letters in our mailbox dozens of times before but always
figured it was junk mail. So I never cared. But this time, I think
about Mom's phone call.

The letter from Taco Bell isn't sealed completely. All the damp
air must have made the glue come undone. I check around, make
sure I'm alone in the mailroom. Then I look inside.

There's a letter apologizing for the bad customer service. Then
there's five vouchers for free meals. My head starts spinning. I'm
tempted to open the other mail. But I don't. Instead, I put back
the letter and vouchers the way they were, lick the envelope, and
seal it closed. When I get home, I leave the mail on the table like
I always do. But I can't keep my mouth shut. As soon as Mom
opens them, I ask, "Did you get those vouchers because you called
and complained?"

Her eyes narrow on me for a second, angry. Then she shrugs.
"Yup. I sure did. Big businesses want to keep their customers

happy. And I'm never happy." Mom smiles, fanning herself with the vouchers.

"What if you got that cashier fired?"

"I didn't give her name," Mom says.

"But isn't that stealing?"

"No, it's not," Mom counters. "Those big companies make millions off of poor people like us 'cause we can't afford to eat anywhere else. So I figure if I'm giving them my money, I should get some back. They can stand to give me a few extra meals every once in a while. They're mega-rich. It's easy really. All I gotta do is call and complain, and they send me free vouchers."

I feel gross. Like I'm walking into those fast food joints and stealing food right off the counter. I wish I'd never looked inside that envelope. Now I know. Our fast food wasn't cheap—it was free. Just like my lunch at school.

INVITE

sit by myself at lunch. The table's on the far edge of the cafeteria. From here, I can see Liam and the other football players. Today, they're all wearing their jerseys, red with white block letters. On the back is a number and a last name.

They're wearing them 'cause today's a pep rally. That's this thing where once a month, the student body (which is a weird way to say all the students at our school) cuts out of seventh period thirty minutes early to go to the gym. Everyone sits on the bleachers and watches. The band plays and the cheerleaders do leaps and pyramids and try to get everyone to stand up. Then the football players come out in their jerseys and everyone claps and cheers them on.

It's kinda like church, but for football instead of God. Though maybe I'm wrong. It's been a long time since I've been to church.

Anyways, I'm sitting alone, feeling embarrassed and dumb. Feeling like I'm not good enough for anything anymore. I'm poor, wear secondhand clothes, can't be on the football team. Just bringing it up got my mom beat up pretty bad. I didn't want that. I just want to be like everyone else.

Thinking about home gets me all worked up and I'm getting real mad and sad at the same time. I don't know how, 'cause they're two different feelings, but I feel them at the same time, and it makes me feel really sick.

I'm staring at my free lunch and I get this flash in my head of me throwing the tray across the cafeteria and just screaming as loud as I can. I don't do it, but that's what I'm thinking. That's when Luke Dodson and this girl walk up with their lunch trays. He asks, "May we join you?"

"Free country." I'm not sure why I said it like that. It's like my mouth is always saying things before I think about it. I sound like a jerk.

Luke Dodson is taller than everyone else in sixth grade. He's wearing a pastel polo shirt and pleated dress pants. He's wearing these real nice shoes made of leather, I think they're called penny loafers, and they don't have a speck of dirt on them. His hair is combed to the side, not a hair out of place. He smiles this big white smile. He's got braces, though I don't know why. His teeth are exactly where they should be. Not like mine, which poke out at all the wrong angles in places.

The girl is dressed real pretty too. She's wearing a checkered dress. It covers a lot of her body, not like how some girls dress at school. When she catches me looking at her, she smiles too. I look down real fast.

Luke puts his hand out. "I'm Luke Dodson." He's kinda formal, which is weird. He wasn't like this last year.

I look at his hand first, to make sure it's not a trick. Some kids put peanut butter in their hands as a gag, or have one of those shock buzzers, like in the cartoons. Luke doesn't though. "I know. We went to fifth grade together. At Lyndon B. Johnson Elementary. You were next door, in Mrs. Shaker's class."

Luke laughs. "Oh, yeah. I thought that was you. Your hair is longer now. Rex Doyle, right?"

"Ogle. But yeah."

The girl says, "I'm Polly Atherton."

I shake her hand too. I think Polly's a funny name, but I don't say that.

"Why are you sitting by yourself?" Polly asks.

I don't know what I expected, but I didn't expect that. Usually kids who don't know each other talk about the weather or about classes or favorite TV shows. They don't ask personal stuff.

"I don't know," I say. Which is true.

"Would you like to sit with us?" Luke says.

"I am sitting with you."

Luke laughs again. "You're funny, Rex. I meant, do you want to sit with the rest of our friends? Over there." He points.

Two tables of students are watching us. I didn't realize we had an audience, and now I feel my face get hot. One of the kids waves.

Todd told me about the kids who sit at those tables. They're real religious. They all sit together, talk about church things and do charity bake sales and stuff. They even pray before they eat. They won't eat a single French fry until they pray. And they don't pray until they're all sitting together.

"I'm OK here," I say.

"Well, we wanted you to know you are welcome to sit with us anytime you want," Luke says.

"Thanks," I say. I'm waiting for him to give me the reason why. People aren't nice for no reason. People are only nice if they want something.

I'm drinking my chocolate milk when Polly asks, "Have you accepted Jesus Christ as your Lord and Savior?"

I do this half-choke, half-snort thing, and chocolate milk sprays out of my nose. I grab my napkin and wipe my face in case any boogers came out with it. "Oh, um . . . uh, no, I guess not."

Luke looks irritated, like Polly beat him to the punch line of a joke he was trying to tell. He tries to smooth it over. "Do you have a house of worship?"

"You mean, like church?" I ask. "Nah. I used to go, with friends, but my mom made me stop. She doesn't like religion too much."

Luke rubs his chin. "I see. That's OK. Everyone has a different path."

"Do you believe in Jesus Christ?" Polly asks.

"Yeah. I think so. I mean, it'd be pretty cool if he did live. He had all those superpowers right?"

"He did," Luke chuckles. "And he is cool. I'm glad you think so too."

"What do you mean *if* he lived. He did live," Polly says, annoyed. "And he's still alive."

"I thought he died."

"But he came back. He resurrected," Polly adds.

"Yeah, but then he died again. Or ascended to heaven?"

I wouldn't bet my life on it, but I know this stuff pretty good. I've read almost the whole Bible by myself.

A lot of it is pretty boring, especially the songs and the poetry parts. But I really like the Adam and Eve stuff, and the Jesus stuff. My favorite is the Book of Revelation, which is about the end of the world, with demons and angels having these big wars. That part is awesome, reminds me of big action movies.

So yeah, I don't remember the exact details, but I know Jesus was crucified, so he could die on purpose for all our sins. I don't know if I could do that though. I'm really scared of dying.

"Yes, but he's still alive!" Polly hisses. She isn't smiling anymore. Her arms are crossed like I said something offensive. "He's everywhere all the time. That's what God is—everything. And everything can't die!"

"So God is like nature?" I ask.

"What? No!" Polly shrieks.

Luke shushes her. He tries to smile again for me. "God is complicated. But you should know, he doesn't want you sitting alone. He loves you."

I don't mean to, but I laugh.

Just for a second.

I honestly don't mean to. I swear. But if God didn't want me sitting by myself, I *wouldn't* be sitting by myself. I mean, they say God is all-powerful. So if I'm sitting by myself, then it's 'cause God *wants* me to sit by myself. Which is pretty awful if you think about it, 'cause no kid should have to feel alone. And if God really does control everything, then that means that God *wants* me to be poor and not be on the football team. It also means God lets people go without meals and get sick and get punched around. And if God's a good guy, he wouldn't let that stuff happen, right?

My mom is real crazy about church stuff. She says religious people are all twisted and evil and manipulative and just want money. I don't believe that. But I also don't know if I believe in the same God they do.

I don't say any of this though. People get real touchy about this kinda stuff. Instead, I say: "I like the idea of God. And Jesus too. I think if he really did die for all of us, so we can go to heaven, that's really nice. But I'm not sure what I believe. 'Cause if God does exist, I'm pretty sure he doesn't like me very much."

"What a horrible thing to say!" Polly's eyes well up with tears.

"God definitely loves you," Luke says. "That's why he sent us to talk to you. You should come to church with us sometime. We go to First Baptist. It's the neatest church in town. We have a drummer and a guitar player, so the singing is really hip. If you come, you can join us for lunch after. Everyone goes."

Luke hands me a church flyer with a drawing of Jesus giving me a thumbs-up. On the back, it has the address, and says, FREE LUNCH! A chill runs up my spine. I don't know why, but I don't trust the word *free* anymore. Lunch here is supposed to be free, but it feels like it costs me a lot.

Then again, I think of the after-church lunches I used to go to with their big buffets, all-you-can-eat style. My mouth starts watering.

I consider it, but I think going to church just for a free meal isn't OK if you don't really believe in God. And like I said, I'm not sure what I believe.

"Thanks," I say. "I'll think about it." I mean it too. Though I already know Mom will say no.

"Cool beans," Luke says. Though I don't know what that means. Luke shakes my hand again. Then he and Polly get up and take their trays back to their group.

Halfway there, Polly turns around, and practically yells, "God *does* love you!"

She seems really upset. I feel bad. Then I realize that while they were talking, I was eating. They weren't. In fact, none of their friends were either. They were waiting for Luke and Polly to return. I watch as the two tables bow their heads and put their hands together. They pray.

When they're done, they finally start eating. I think praying is pretty cool. I haven't done it in a long time. I got tired of having all my prayers ignored. Maybe I'll try it again. Not before I eat though. Usually when I'm hungry, praying doesn't seem all that important.

BRUISES

walk home from the bus stop with Brad. He's whistling this Metallica song he loves. I can't whistle. When I try, I end up just blowing air and it doesn't make any sound.

He suddenly grabs me and points down at the sidewalk. "Dude, watch out! Step on a crack, and break your mother's back."

"Huh?"

"It's bad luck to step on a crack, dumbass. You could kill your mother."

"I've never heard that before. That can't be true."

"Your risk, man," Brad says. His mom died when Benny was born. I start to wonder how many sidewalk cracks I've stepped on. I'm so lost in thought, I almost do it again. My foot is half an inch above a crack, and I freak. What if this is like a real curse? I half jump, half twist to the side to dodge the crack, and I trip over my other foot. I fall real hard and skin my knee. It starts bleeding everywhere.

Brad laughs. "You're almost as stupid as Benny."

Brad's right. I am stupid. But even though I may not like my mom, I don't want her back broken. Maybe Sam's though. Would serve him right for hitting me and Mom.

I limp up the stairs to our second-floor apartment. I use my key to unlock the deadbolt. Inside, Ford's sitting on the floor watching cartoons and chewing the head off my Princess Leia figure. "Stop! That's mine!" I snap, grabbing it from him.

"Mine!" he yells back.

"No. This is *mine*. All the *Star Wars* stuff in *my* room, that's *mine*."

"No, mine!" he shouts. "Mom gave me." She's always giving him my stuff, even when I hide it in the top of the closet.

My blood boils. I'm ready to scream at her. I could've broken her back, but scraped my knee to save her, and this is my thanks?

I stomp toward the bedroom. The door is closed. Is she taking a nap? With Ford alone in the living room? Ford's only two and a half. You have to really watch him. Especially since we have a second-floor apartment and a balcony with big railings that he could fall through. Now I'm really pissed. Ford could have gotten hurt.

I'm steaming with anger. I raise my fist to beat on the door when I hear it—the crying.

Only it's not a soft cry. It's thick, heavy with pain.

Sobbing. Moaning.

I get all torn up inside. Sometimes, I hate my mom so much. Like when she's hitting me. Or just being really cruel. But when she cries? I can't. I just can't hate her 'cause it's like she's hurting so bad I don't understand.

I knock real gentle and open the door. "Mom?"

She doesn't seem to notice.

"You OK?" I ask.

Her face is buried in the pillow. She hits it twice, then lets out this wail. This horrible gut-wrenching wail. I've only heard her cry like this a few times before, like after my sister died. Like she's in the most pain in the whole world.

I don't know how to fix it, how to make her feel better. So I sit at the edge of the bed. I put my hand on her foot, so she knows I'm there. I don't say anything. I let her cry.

Outside the window, this big blue sky is glowing with sun. In the living room, Ford's cartoons make funny, happy noises. The smell of fresh-baked bread or cookies wafts in from outside. Like the whole world just goes on, no matter who is hurting.

Mom's bedroom is empty except for the mattress and the box spring under it, and the metal frame under that. Some clothes are in the closet on wire hangers. There's a fan in the corner. That's it. No photos. No albums. No books. No jewelry box with a ballerina in it. No tin of little keepsakes. My mom doesn't have anything.

The most colorful thing in the room are Mom's bruises. Deep sunrise purple, bright stone turquoise, shocking bumblebee yellow. Lumps adorn her legs and arms, the hues so brilliant, they could be shiny new tattoos. But I know from experience they must be two days old. I didn't even know she and Sam had a fight this time. It must have happened while I was at school. I hate that he hits her.

"Say you love me," Mom whispers.

"I do." I smooth her hair back. She crawls into my lap and sobs. I think about the first time she did this. When I was five years old, and my dad left. She did it a lot then. More when her next boyfriend left. Again the first time Sam really roughed her up.

"Say it again," she whispers. "Tell me you love me. Say you'll never leave."

"I love you. I'm not going anywhere." I say it, but I don't mean it. If I could, if I had money, I would probably run away and never come back. I'd take Ford with me.

Another bruise wraps around her neck like wallpaper, only instead of flowers, it's decorated with fingerprints of crimson and purple. Hate bubbles up from my stomach, burning my throat like acid. I hate Sam. I really do. Sometimes I want him dead. Or at least in jail.

He's been before. Twice. Just for a few days though. It didn't stick. I don't know why he has to hit my mom. Or me. It doesn't make him tough. It doesn't make him better than anybody. It just makes him a jerk.

Mom sits up. Only, she doesn't look like a mom. Or even an adult. She reminds me of a little girl, six or seven maybe. Her face swollen from crying. Her eyes all innocent, scared. She looks at me like she's never seen me before.

Snot drips from her nose, down to her lip. She sniffs, wiping with the back of her hand. Then she smiles. It looks weird on her wet face. "How was school today?"

"Fine, I guess," I say, confused. "Are you OK?"

"Of course I'm OK!" she says, hopping off the bed with a spring in her step. She goes into the hall closet and picks up the laundry basket. "Do you have any dirty clothes in your room? I'm doing darks."

"You were crying pretty hard. Do you want to talk?"

"I *wasn't* crying!" she yells, rolling her eyes, like what I've said is ridiculous. Which confuses me more, 'cause her face is still wet, her eyes beet red.

"Your leg," she points. Then she starts laughing. Hysterically. Like my bloody knee is the funniest thing she's ever seen in her entire life.

After all this time, her sudden mood shifts still catch me off guard. It's like I have two different mothers living in the same body. One who is happy and warm with Sam or Ford, and one who is the opposite, usually with me.

Mom laughs and laughs and laughs. Until she slumps against the wall and starts crying again.

I sit down next to her, not sure what to do. My scraped knee has bled all down my leg. My sock and shoe are glistening red. I forgot about myself when I started taking care of Mom. This isn't the first time either.

I can't help thinking it, but I wish I had a different mom. One who took care of me, rather than the other way around.

BUGS

"Why are the windows closed?" Mom asks when she wakes up.

"I was cold," I say.

"It's going to be a hot day. Keep them open," she snaps, opening the windows again. "Better that the house is cold now so it's only cool later."

"Can't we just run the AC?" I ask.

"Are you going to pay for it?"

I shake my head.

"That's what I thought." I hate when Mom wakes up mad. That means her mood's gonna stay bad the whole day. She goes and checks the thermostat, to make sure I didn't turn the heater on or anything. There's a little piece of tape over the thermostat, a reminder for me and Sam not to touch it. When she sees the tape is there, she gives me a warning glare, then goes back to her room.

I return to my homework. On Saturdays, I try to get ahead on my studying so the week isn't too crazy. Right now, I'm doing math on the couch.

Anyways, there's this *bzzz bzzz bzzz bzzz* sound. I look up and it's one of those big red wasps, bouncing against the inside of the window trying to get out. When those suckers sting you, it's like getting stabbed by fire. I know 'cause I've been stung a bunch of times. Hurts like crazy.

The *bzzz bzzz bzzz bzzz* keeps on for a while. Finally, I get up.

All slow like, I pull the cord that lifts up the blinds. All the windows, and the balcony door, are open. But this stupid wasp chooses the one closed window in the whole apartment. It's the one window that won't open. We all tried to get it open a bunch of different ways, but it's painted shut or broken or something.

The wasp finally gets smart (or so I think) and flies away from the window. It does one circle of the living room, then goes right back to the same closed window. Dumb bug.

Vista Nueva is full of all kinds of insects. The courtyard is full of ants, the bushes full of wasps and dirt daubers. Mosquitoes are everywhere when it's hot. Flies stay over by the dumpsters, but in whole swarms. Hundreds of daddy longlegs spiders live in the utility boxes. Sometimes Benny and I go look at them, just 'cause it's so creepy to see so many in one place. But the worst are the cockroaches. They usually come out after dark.

It doesn't matter how clean Mom and I keep our apartment, the bugs still find a way in.

The *bzzz bzzz bzzz bzzz* sound keeps going on. The wasp keeps flying at the glass over and over and over, like it doesn't know the difference between glass and open air. Maybe it doesn't. I don't know. Instead of flying to any of the open windows, it just keeps going *bzzz bzzz bzzz bzzz* against the glass.

It's driving me nuts.

Sure, the sound is annoying. But it makes me crazy 'cause if the dang thing doesn't figure it out, it'll die. I'm not being dramatic. It happens to bugs all the time. They come in, zip around, then try to fly out the locked window. They just bounce off the glass, *bzzz bzzz bzzz bzzz*, over and over. They always end up dead, cause they can't eat or drink I guess. The whole windowsill is a graveyard. Flies. Mosquitoes. Bees. They eventually give up and never move again.

"Stop being stupid," I say out loud. Like the wasp understands. "Just fly to the window."

I roll up some of my homework papers and try to shoo the wasp to the next open window. It won't go. The third time I do this, it flies at my face like its gonna sting me. "Screw you then!"

I go back to my homework.

It's still making the *bzzz bzzz bzzz bzzz* sound and making me crazy, so I just go to my room to do homework.

If that bug wants to keep doing the same thing over and over and over and over till it dies, go ahead.

Idiot.

———

THAT NIGHT, I STAY OVER AT BRAD AND BENNY'S. WE WATCH THIS movie *Mad Max*, with all these people living in a desert 'cause humans bombed the cities or something. It's pretty good. The next morning, when I come home, the wasp is dead. Lying on the windowsill with the others.

I stare at it, its body not moving. Its legs curl in, fetal, like a baby sleeping.

This big dread comes over me. Like I'm all alone, and cold inside my body, and I want to run into Mom's arms and just cry. It's so stupid. So, *so, so* stupid. I know that in my brain. But I can't stop this horrible feeling, and it grows inside me. I fill up with guilt and regret. 'Cause I could have saved the wasp if I really tried. I shoulda tried harder. I could have used a drinking glass and a notecard to capture it, get it outside. But I didn't. I gave up too fast and now this living thing isn't alive anymore.

It's dead.

And it's my fault.

Carefully, I pick it up. I take the wasp's body outside and bury it. I think about praying, but stop myself. If God cared, he would have made the wasp smarter, so it wasn't stuck, bouncing against the glass, trying to get outside to the sunshine and the rest of the world. God would have helped it, given it a good life. But he didn't.

God doesn't care. Not about the little guys, like the wasp. Like me.

———

THAT NIGHT, AS I DRIFT OFF TO SLEEP, I WONDER ABOUT THE WASP, if there's an insect heaven, if it's the same as human heaven. I imagine it would be. Heaven should be like Earth, right? Except everyone is happy. I like that idea.

When I dream, I dream that I'm the one trapped behind the window. I'm hitting it, trying to escape, but the glass won't break. Outside, all these kids from school are laughing at me. I want to cry, but I don't. Instead, I get real angry and start screaming.

Then my legs feel all weird, like they're being tickled with a feather. Or birds are pulling at the little blond leg hairs starting to sprout down there. Then I have the same weird sensation on my cheek, like a mouse is dancing on my face.

That's when I wake up.

"*ARGGGHHHH!*" I scream. Sitting up, two cockroaches fall off my face. There's a few more on my legs and arms. I don't know what they were doing. Were they laying eggs in my mouth? Were they trying to eat me while I slept?

I'm freaking out so hard, I don't even realize I'm still screaming. Not until Mom and Sam run into my room. The second Mom turns on the light, a dozen roaches skitter and scurry toward the crack in the wall.

Mom's screams match my own. She and I hug each other, jumping up and down, shrieking. Sam picks up my sleeping bag and slaps it. More insects scurry out of it.

"That's it! That is the final straw! We are moving out of this dump!" Mom screams. "I've had it! *I've. Had. It!*"

I'm shivering, from fear I guess, holding on to my mom. Sam looks over at me and pushes me away from her, "Q-q-quit b-b-being a sissy."

"He's *not* a sissy!" Mom yells. "He was just attacked by cockroaches."

"He w-w-wasn't attacked," Sam says. "Th-th-they're h-harmless b-bugs."

"How do you know?" I ask. I want to say, *You didn't even finish high school*. But I don't.

They argue for a minute about moving. Mom hates it here. Sam says we don't have money to move. Finally, Sam says, "Sh-shut up, w-woman. I'm tired."

Mom hugs me. "You OK?"

I nod. She looks me in the eye and shivers, doing a whole-body shake. "Bugs are so gross." We both laugh.

For a minute, I see my mom. The one who loves me. I want this moment to last. But it's late. Mom follows Sam back to their room, with the actual bed, where Ford slept through the whole thing.

And I'm all alone again.

When I turn off the light and go to lie down, my heart starts racing. There's no furniture in my room, but it feels claustrophobic. Like the bugs are still everywhere. They don't like the light, so I turn it back on. After a few minutes of watching to see if any are around, I crawl back into my sleeping bag, zipping it all the way closed with me inside.

THE NEXT DAY AT SCHOOL, MR. CHANG STARTS SCIENCE CLASS with a chapter on insects. I shiver just thinking about last night.

"Here's a fun fact," Mr. Chang says, "if humans bomb the planet with their nuclear arsenal, the only life left on Earth will be cockroaches. Only they can survive the toxic fallout."

Someone screams, "Gross!"

Someone else shouts, "Disgusting!"

I want to tell the class my story. That'd really creep them out. But I know rich people don't have cockroaches. That's a poor-

people problem. I don't want people knowing how poor I am. So
I keep my mouth closed.

Then I think about it: If the world gets bombed, cockroaches
will take over the planet—like they have my apartment complex.
So yeah. Guess that means if I figure out a way to survive the radia-
tion, I'll be right at home.

HALLOWEEN

— ⬝

At school, we get to wear costumes. I know all the cool kids are going to dress up. So I want to dress up too.

I ask Mom if I can buy a costume. She laughs. "Sure, I'll buy you one. If you give me the money for it." She knows I don't have any.

I'm all upset. It's not fair. Other kids probably don't even think about money. They just tell their parents what they want, and they get it. It's not like that in my house.

Guess I have to do what I always do for Halloween. I have to make my own costume.

Last year, I mixed green paint into Elmer's glue and coated my whole body with it. When the glue dries, it cracks, looks like skin peeling off. I got some clothes from a penny sale, cut them up, and rubbed them with dirt like I crawled out of a grave. Then I went as a zombie.

Another time, I built a robot costume with cardboard boxes, foil, wire coat hangers, and some flashlights I borrowed. When I was little, I just covered myself in flour, 'cause it makes everything

white, like a ghost. You can make all kinds of costumes if you use
crap from around your house or from Goodwill.

But I'm not a kid anymore. I'm in middle school now, so
I have to make it real good. I start looking around the apartment
for stuff. There's cotton balls and Kleenex, so I could make a
cloud costume, but that's really dumb. (Maybe I'll do that for
Ford. If he asks nicely.) There's not much in our place, so I go out
to the dumpsters. I know that sounds gross, but most stuff is in
plastic bags so it's not as dirty as it sounds. I kind of peek in and
look around. I'm not going to hop in unless there's something
really rad.

Sometimes, Benny jumps right in and starts ripping open
trash bags. He's found some neat stuff like old flags and broken
furniture that looks like ninja weapons, but mostly he just finds
food leftovers, cigarette ashes, and beer bottles. That's what
makes dumpsters stink so bad.

When I don't spot anything, I check behind the dumpster.
There's some broken electronics, wood scraps, an old coffee table
covered in stains, and a bag of clothes. Inside, there's a pair of
jeans, some black boots, and some flannel shirts. One of them
has a big stain that looks like blood. It gives me an idea.

In this one horror movie series, *Friday the 13th*, there's this
guy who wears a hockey mask and uses a machete to go around
hacking up sexy teenagers at some kind of summer camp. I've
never been to a summer camp, but Jason Voorhees would be a
cool costume. In middle school, you can't dress up as a cartoon
character or anything kindergarten like that. I need something
that other people won't make fun of.

Plus, Jason is kinda an easy costume to make. Especially now that I have the right clothes. After I wash them, I paint the jeans and shirt in some mud, so it looks like I crawled out of the lake. Then I draw a machete on a cardboard box and cut it out. I wrap the blade part in foil, and the handle in brown packing tape. For the hockey mask, I do the same thing, except I paint it white and black. I skip lunch one day, going to hang out in the art classroom instead, so I can use the paints there. Then I add a strap to the mask, so it stays on my face.

Benny and Brad make about a gallon of fake blood from corn syrup and red dye, and let me have some. So I splash that on my jacket, hands, and the machete. My costume turns out really good.

"Who are you supposed to be?" Mom asks.

"Jason Voorhees. From *Friday the 13th*."

"That's a horror movie," she says. "How do you even know what that is? You're not allowed to watch that crap."

"Yeah, but kids at school talk about it."

Mom doesn't let me watch horror movies. She says they're evil, that I shouldn't see all that violence. Doesn't make a lot of sense, coming from her, 'cause she hits me all the time.

It's a dumb rule. Which is why I ignore it. I watch scary movies, just without permission. Brad's always renting them. They're not even that scary. Monsters and vampires and witches and stuff don't scare me. Not even when they're killing people. I feel like stuff in real life is way scarier.

Except for zombies. They really freak me out. 'Cause I feel like they could really happen in the real world.

Anyways. I'm glad I made the costume. When I get to school,

everyone is dressed up. Some kids look like popular presidents or famous movie people. One girl is dressed as her favorite singer. Some students dress up real funny, like hamburgers or other food and stuff. Others are the usual monsters. My favorite one is this one girl wearing a prom dress and like a ton of blood. She says it's from a famous movie based on a book by Stephen King. I make a mental note to find the book.

In first period, this one guy has cereal glued all over his clothes, and a plastic knife stabbed through a Froot Loops box on his head. I don't get it until he tells someone, "I'm a *cereal* killer." I can't stop laughing. That's really smart.

I think when people wear masks, they're different. I mean, everyone's smiling and laughing and trying to guess who's who behind what mask. No one is sure who I am. People keep asking, "Who are you?" I just shrug and raise my machete like I'm going to kill them. They usually laugh. I kinda like people not knowing who I am. I feel more free or something. Like I'm not me. Like I'm someone else.

At least, that's how I feel until third period. Mrs. Winstead says, "No masks in my class. Take them off. All of you."

Then she calls out our names one by one. Our homework was to write a short Halloween story to read in front of the class. Usually I hate speaking, but I wrote a really good story. When it's my turn, I'm all excited to read it. Mrs. Winstead stops my turn after I read the first paragraph. "You can't read about killing people, Mr. Ogle."

"They're not dead-dead. They're ghosts. Well, demon-ghosts. It's a Halloween story. It's supposed to be spooky."

"Abject foolishness. Not in my class. Have a seat."

I'm real pissed off. The assignment was only for one page, but I wrote six. Everyone else has some dumb story about trick-or-treating or a cat scared of a pumpkin. Mine has a haunted house, and all these really horrible demons killing people, and only one girl surviving, just like a movie. Mrs. Winstead—a real-life witch—doesn't let me get to the surprise ending. No one is really dead. It's all a big prank.

For the rest of class, I just sit there, arms crossed. She'll probably give me a bad grade, even though my story was better than anyone else's. I had to handwrite the whole thing twice, just so there were no errors in it. When the bell rings, I'm glad to get out of there and put my mask back on.

On the way to lunch, Liam calls out. "Ogle! Hey, is that you? I heard your costume was awesome. And it is. Holy cow. You made that? So cool. Looks just like the movie."

"Thanks," I say.

"Do you like my costume?" He's wearing his red-and-white jersey over his shoulder pads, along with his cleats and helmet— his whole football uniform. He even has a football in one hand.

I say, "I don't get it."

"I'm a football player."

"But you *are* a football player. That's not a costume."

"Sure it is," he says. I still don't get it, but he changes the subject. "Sucks that you didn't join the football team. I never see you. Maybe try out next semester. I can coach you before. Teach you everything I'm learning."

"Thanks." That's really nice of him. I'd like that. But I don't want to think about what would happen if I asked Mom to play football again.

"We should hang sometime," he says.

I shake my head. "Sure. When's good?"

He shrugs. "I don't know. I'm always at football practice. When I'm not, Dad makes me practice with him."

"Let me know," I say. I mean it too. I miss hanging out with Liam. Todd too. Even Zach.

This girl walks by. I think her name is Amelia, but I'm not sure. She's dressed as this yellow slinky alien from a candy commercial. When she sees Liam, she gives him this little wave, the way girls do when they have a crush.

Liam smirks. "Nice costume! You look like a giant condom."

I don't really get it, but I laugh anyway. 'Cause Liam is laughing real hard, like whatever he said is hysterical.

But then something awful happens. Amelia's eyes get this really horrible hurt look, and start to well up. I hope she won't but she does. She bursts into tears. She runs away, down the hall.

This real bad sick feeling takes hold in my stomach. Like I'm gonna puke. Liam's still laughing. He even holds up his hand for a high-five. Real slow, I high-five him. I don't know why.

"Dude, that was hilarious," he says.

"I guess." But I didn't know Amelia was gonna cry. I didn't know it'd upset her so much, us laughing at her. People have done worse stuff to me, and I didn't cry. But Amelia and I aren't the same. I don't know her life. I hate that I hurt this girl I don't even know.

Especially 'cause I know how it feels, to have people laugh at you.

It sucks.

Then I see the principal barreling toward us. Everyone knows him cause he's the tallest person in the school by like six inches. Usually he's always smiling, but this time he looks real mad, his hands balled into fists. We've never met but somehow he knows our names. "Liam! Rex! Did you say something obscene to a young lady just now?"

"No," Liam says.

I shake my head.

"Did you say her costume looked like a condom?" the principal asks.

Liam shrugs. "Well, it does!"

"You owe that girl an apology," the principal says. I'm ready to apologize immediately. I feel horrible, the sick feeling still rolling around in my gut like ocean water. With other students gathering around us, whispering, my stomach tightens, a little puke comes up, burning my throat. I swallow it back down.

"I'm not apologizing," Liam says. "It was just a joke."

"Do you want detention?" the principal asks.

Liam groans. "No! God! Chill, man." The principal walks us around the corner to where Amelia is crying.

"I'm sorry," I say.

Liam is about to apologize until he sees his football friends watching. Instead of apologizing, he says, "I'm not."

The principal grabs Liam's arm. "Apologize this instant."

"Fine! I'm sorry, Amelia—" Liam starts. "Sorry your costume's so ugly."

The principal loses it, dragging Liam toward his office. Liam's laughing the whole way, even high-fiving some of his football buddies.

There's a crowd now, and they're all left staring at me and Amelia.

"I really am sorry," I say. I mean it. I honestly do. I hate when people get hurt. No one should hurt. My voice is really low when I add, "It's a good costume. It is."

A few fresh tears run down Amelia's wet cheeks. She chokes out, "It's all my nana could afford." Some of the football players are snickering and pointing at her. She breaks through the crowd and disappears into the girls' bathroom.

Not the football players, but everyone else is looking at me, like I really am a killer, not just dressed like one. They whisper and point and glare at me. I deserve it.

No wonder God hates me. I am awful. Other kids at school are dressed like werewolves and Frankensteins and stuff, but those're just costumes.

I really am a monster.

WEIRD KID

"**R**ex Ogle," I repeat.

The cafeteria cashier is trying to find my name in the red folder. She licks her finger, then turns the pages one by one. She is squinting at the list of names. It annoys me that she still has no idea who I am — even after two months of going through this Monday through Friday. I don't understand how people can be so stupid.

"Rex Fogle?" she asks.

"Rex *Ogle*," I moan, "like it is every day."

Her wrinkles tighten around her old eyes, her squint shifting into a glare. "You are very rude."

Then I feel all bad. She's not Mexican, but she's still old, and that reminds me of my abuela or my other grandma. Part of me wants to apologize. The other part of me just doesn't understand why she can't remember my name.

Finally she finds my name on the Free Lunch list. She makes the checkmark next to my name. I say, "Look, I'm sorry—"

Curtly, she says, "Next."

Now I'm kinda annoyed and mad. I was trying to apologize. I wasn't even *that* rude to begin with. The things I could have said, the things rolling around in my head? It probably would give her a heart attack if I said them. But I don't say any of it. Even though it's on the tip of my tongue, like it's trying to get out.

I hate the things in my head.

The stuff I think sometimes? It's real awful and dark. It's evil.

It's almost like the stuff that happens at home, it gets in my head like an infection. Like when one kid gets chicken pox, everyone around them gets it. Except instead of little itchy red dots, I hear Mom and Sam in my head. The stuff they scream at each other. She says these cruel things. Then he says real horrible stuff back. And it just gets worse. Escalates till the hitting.

Sam calls me and Mom names, like, every day. Me? I'm a sissy. Or a queer. Or runt. Or pussy. Or wetback. The stuff he calls Mom? I don't wanna repeat it.

So when a person—especially a woman—is rude or mean to me, it's like some part of me wants to call them those names too.

I don't. But it takes all this effort not to. 'Cause I don't want to be like Sam. Though I think part of me already is. Otherwise, why would I think that sorta terrible stuff?

I'm eating my lunch at a table by myself, thinking about all these things, wishing I were anyone else. I'm kinda picking at my food, cause I feel stomach-sick, even though I'm really hungry. And I'm all in my head, so I almost don't notice someone sit down across from me without asking.

I look up. I don't even know this guy. He's short and white, and has a funny bowl-shaped haircut with brown hair. I check up and down the table to see if he's made a mistake or is lost or something.

He says, "The system sucks."

I ask, "What system?"

"The social setup where students are hustled into lines like cattle, then forced to find seats that make them feel insecure and unwanted. It's as though the principals and teachers want us to fight for social standing, or choose to be placed in a box that defines us." He forks a bit of peas and mashed potatoes into his mouth. He chews slowly, swallows, then continues. "Band geeks. Theatre students. Eighth-grade jocks. Seventh-grade jocks. Cheerleaders. Goth kids. Heavy-metal wannabes—"

I wonder if he's one of the church kids. Maybe Luke Dodson sent him to try and get me to go to church again.

"Which are you?" I ask.

"I don't have a label," he says. "I'm just me."

"Oh." That's all I say.

We both eat a little.

Then he starts again, "I bet there are cameras hidden all over this cafeteria. They're recording us, and we're all part of some big social experiment, conducted by the government. Psychiatrists are probably watching us right now, trying to decipher the riddle of today's youth."

I say, "You're kinda weird, huh?"

"Weird is just a label people put on people who are brilliant."

People say I'm weird sometimes. I wonder if that makes me brilliant too. But I don't think really smart people grow up in trailer parks and crappy apartments. Or if they do, no one ever finds out they're smart, 'cause they're too busy trying to find their next meal and pay their bills and stuff.

The weird kid and I both eat for a while. Then I ask, "You really think they're watching us?"

He shrugs. "It wouldn't be the strangest thing the government's ever done. During the Vietnam War, they tested chemical warfare on their own soldiers. It was called Agent Orange. This band R.E.M. made it into a song. Look it up."

"Why would they do that?"

"R.E.M. makes all kinds of political songs."

"No, I mean the government. Why would they hurt their own people?"

"Easier to monitor them, I guess. It's always easier to hurt the ones you're closest to, the ones you love," he says.

Makes me think of Mom and Sam. But if they love me, they don't say it.

"I'm Ethan."

"Rex."

He nods. "Cool name. It has an *x* in it. Like *X-Men*."

"What's that?"

"Awww, man! You don't know? It's only like the coolest comic book out there." Ethan starts digging through his backpack. He pulls out a bunch of comics, each in a plastic sleeve with a piece of cardboard behind it, to protect it I guess. The covers have all these folks in bright-colored Spandex fighting one another. Liam and Zach always said comic books are for nerds. So I never read them. But looking at these, I like the colors. The art's pretty cool too.

"What are those about?"

"The X-Men are sworn to protect a world that fears and hates them," Ethan says. "They're mutants. That means they have special powers, like controlling the weather or shooting blasts out of their eyes or having healing factors and adamantium claws. Well, actually, technically, Wolverine's adamantium *isn't* part of his mutant ability. The government added that later, against his will."

"You don't like the government, do you?"

"I don't trust them," Ethan says. "Distrust is healthy."

I don't know what that even means. This kid's super weird. But he does seem smart, and he knows a bunch of stuff.

"If you could have a mutant superpower, what would it be?" Ethan asks.

"I don't know," I say. I think about it. "I think it'd be cool to move stuff without touching it. I saw that in a movie once. This chick was making stuff fly all over the room with her mind."

"That's telekinesis," Ethan says. "Good choice. I'm glad you didn't say you'd want to fly. Everyone says that. That's such an easy one."

"But if I had telekinesis, I could just move myself around. Then I could fly too," I say.

"Excellent point!" Ethan says, getting all excited.

"What superpower would you have?"

Ethan rubs his hands together. "I'm glad you asked. My favorite character is Iceman. He can freeze stuff, and make ice slides. But I don't know if that's the power I'd want. There're so many things you have to consider first. Do you want powers to fight villains, or make the world a better place or simply to impress girls—" Ethan talks for a long time. I'm not sure if he actually answers the question.

While he's talking, I think how cool it'd be if I did have super-powers. If I turned invisible, I could take my free lunch without having to deal with the cashier. (It's not stealing if it's free, right?) Or if I could teleport, I could just grab my lunch and vanish off to some other place to eat it. I wonder if being super rich is a super-power. I'd take that too.

"You can borrow one of my comics," Ethan says. "But you have to promise to take care of it."

For a minute, I get weirded out. Why's he being so nice to me? Why'd he sit here? What's he want? Point-blank, I ask, "Are you one of those church kids? Coming over here to get me to go to church?"

Ethan starts laughing. "I don't go to church. I'm agnostic."

"Is agnostic a religion?"

"Hah! No. It means I don't believe, but I also don't *not* believe."

"Huh?" I say.

"I'm waiting for proof," Ethan says. "Like, if God shows up and says, 'Hey I'm real, check out my cool powers that prove I'm God,' then I'll believe. But until then, I'm undecided."

"Oh."

"Why do you ask?" Ethan says.

"You sat down and started being really nice," I say. "Usually that means people want something."

"See? I told you," Ethan says. "Distrust *is* healthy. You're being cautious. That's a survival skill a lot of people don't have."

"It is?"

Ethan nods.

The bell rings.

"Time for class." Ethan puts his comics back in his backpack. All but one. He slides it across the table to me. "Here, take it. Just for borrow though. You have to give it back. How about tomorrow? We can sit together again. If you want."

For the first time all lunch, Ethan breaks eye contact. He looks at the table. Nervous. Like he's scared of my answer.

Then it dawns on me. Ethan wants someone to sit with. Just like I do. I wonder if he doesn't have friends 'cause he didn't get on the football team either. Or maybe he's just a total weirdo. Then again, who am I? I'm a total poor kid.

"Sure," I say. "See ya tomorrow. Same table?"

Ethan smiles. "Same bat time, same bat place."

I have no idea what that means, but I start laughing.

HOME ALONE

"There's milk and cereal and twenty dollars on the kitchen counter, so you can order pizza one night," Mom says. She is putting clothes into a plastic grocery bag. "No friends in the house. And no strangers either."

I roll my eyes. "I'm not stupid. Why would I invite strangers over?"

"You can go outside, but stay in the apartment complex," Mom adds.

"I know all of this already," I say, wishing she would shut up. I'm trying to watch cartoons, but she keeps talking.

"Are you *listening*?" she hisses, voice raised.

"Yes!" I yell back. "You go away all the time, I know what to do!" And I do. Every few months, Mom and Sam go on these little trips outta town. They leave me and Ford home.

Some kids might be scared to be left alone. I'm not. Not anymore, anyways.

Probably 'cause the first time really freaked me out. Ford

was barely a year old and I was only nine. We'd just moved to Birmingham the week before so I didn't know anybody. Mom said they were going to be gone just overnight. Instead, they were gone for almost four days. That doesn't seem like a long time now, but when you're nine, it feels like an eternity.

There was no phone number to reach Mom. We didn't have a phone anyways, so I couldn't even call the cops if something bad happened. Which it kinda did. The second night, someone banged on the door at like two in the morning. Whoever he was, he was yelling and kicking the door. I thought he was going to bust in and rob the place or kill me. Eventually, he went away, but I didn't sleep that night. Or the next.

On the third day, we ran out of food. Ford wouldn't stop crying, he was so hungry. I didn't know what to do. I ended up knocking on a bunch of random doors till someone answered. I asked to borrow bread from this guy who looked at me like I was crazy. I'd never been so ashamed.

When Mom and Sam walked in the door, I started screaming at them. Mom slapped me so hard my teeth hurt. Then she was shouting, asking what was wrong with me. I started crying really hard. I didn't understand it, but it was like I was real mad at them, but also real glad they came home at the same time. When I was younger I cried a lot. I don't know why I was like that, but I don't do it now. I almost never cry.

All the feelings that make me sad, I lock those away, deep down inside, in a safe that I drop into a dark well in my soul. Then I bury the hole and try to forget about it.

Mom grabs my head and screams right in my ear. *"Did you hear me?!"*

"Goddammit! That hurts!" I shout back, grabbing my ear.

Mom raises her eyebrows and smirks, like she just won a prize. "You'll go to hell for saying that, you little heathen."

"Can't be worse than here," I mutter. But I feel this big well of guilt fill up my gut. I don't know if I believe in God, but I know you're not supposed say his name like a curse word. I start to worry that I am going to hell for this one mistake.

As Mom puts her bags by the door, Ford starts crying. "No! Don' go! Pease, don'! I be good. Pomise."

"H-h-hey, st-stop crying. Rex is st-staying here with you," Sam says. He picks up Ford, giving him a big hug. I see it, and know he's never hugged me like that. Neither has my own dad. Not that I know of.

Sam puts Ford in my lap. I hold him, but Ford flops and squirms and pushes, bucking like a bronco, trying to get away from me. Mom pets Ford's hair and kisses his cheeks and his forehead.

I ask, "Can you at least tell me where you're going?"

"Only a few hours away. Don't worry," Mom says.

"Why can't Ford and I go too?"

"'Cause we're going to be working the whole time! It won't be fun for you! Why do you have to be so difficult all the time?" she shrieks. She calms down. "You know, most kids would love to be left home alone for a whole weekend."

"I would if I weren't babysitting," I say. Mom raises the back of her hand fast. I flinch. That seems to satisfy her. I hate that I flinched, but I hate more that she enjoyed it. I ask, "You'll be back on Sunday?"

Mom groans. "I already said we would. Quit being a baby. You're going to have a blast. Now, come give me a hug."

"I can't." Ford is still crying and thrashing, wanting to go with them. Instead Mom leans down and gives us this awkward hug from above. For me, hugs are few and far between. It feels weird.

As the door closes behind our parents, Ford starts screeching. He's so loud, you'd think he was being attacked by wild animals. When I finally let him go, he runs at the door. He slams into it and bounces off. I try not to laugh. It's funny but it's not. It's like *America's Funniest Home Videos*, the way he rebounds off the door. He sits there on the floor, all these tears in his big blue eyes. It's like I can tell he's feeling what I'm feeling. Like they're leaving us. And they might not come back.

I try to distract him. First with some books, then with toys. I try to play with him, but he won't have it. So I turn up the TV volume and put on some baby cartoons. All the singing and repeating stuff on those shows is super annoying, but Ford loves it. Finally, slowly, my little brother comes over and crawls into my lap.

The sun glints off his wet cheeks. Droplets are trapped on his long lashes. When he's sad like this, I get this horrible ache in my chest, and my face gets all hot around my eyes, and my head starts hurting. I don't know what to call it, but I hate it. I hate that our parents make us feel this way.

After a few minutes, I get up, and Ford gets this look on his face like I'm leaving too. "I'm not going anywhere," I say. "I was gonna get you chocolate milk. Want some? I'll make it for you." He nods his head.

That night, I make Eggs & Wieners. It's a recipe I made up.

Sliced hot dogs and scrambled eggs with some pepper. It's really salty. Ford loves it. After he falls asleep, I watch some dumb movie about art thieves.

We'd probably watch TV all weekend, but it's hard to find anything good 'cause we don't have cable. For a while we only got two channels. Until I built an antenna system out of wires and foil and metal coat hangers. Now we get six channels. Seven channels, if someone holds one end of the foil up in the air by the window, but that's annoying.

———

ON SATURDAY, THE APARTMENT COURTYARD IS BUSY. THESE little kids, Ryan and Vanessa, are building with big plastic blocks on the sidewalk. Vanessa's mom is watching while she sits in a folding lawn chair, reading a book. Kids my age are chasing after one another, playing a game of hide-and-seek freeze tag. Ford is gripping two of my fingers with his five tiny fingers. In his other hand, he is holding his favorite red fire truck.

"Play fire trucks?" he asks me, except Ford always pronounces "*tr*" like "*f*." So instead of saying "truck," he's says the F-word. I try not to laugh.

"Yeah, go play," I say.

He joins Ryan and Vanessa. I stand guard. Vanessa's mom gazes up from her book, giving me a nod. I give it back.

Benny runs past me, chased by Brad. Brad tackles him, shoving his face into the dirt, saying, "You're it, goober."

Benny dusts himself off, and asks, "You gonna play with us? You can be on my team."

I want to, but I look at Ford. He seems so small and fragile. Like he could break. "I can't. I have to watch my brother."

Vanessa's mom says, "I can watch him if you want."

I shake my head no. "Thanks though."

Benny shrugs, rejoining the others. I hate that I can't join my friends. That I have to skip fun 'cause my parents left me in charge. With Mom and Sam gone, Ford is my responsibility. If anything happened to him—

I try not to think about that. I have crazy nightmares about a kidnapper showing up and stealing Ford. Sam and Mom practically murder me, saying it's all my fault. And it is, 'cause I wasn't watching Ford when I should have been. I don't know why I dream about stuff like that, but I do, and I wake up feeling real awful.

"*Woo-woo-woo-woo*," Ford says, making his fire-truck sounds. "Watch out for my fire truck!" Except he doesn't say truck. He says the other word.

Vanessa's mom drops her book.

I try not to crack up. Vanessa's mom doesn't think it's as funny as I do. I shrug, saying, "Sorry. He has a lisp."

———

FOR DINNER, I ORDER A LARGE PEPPERONI PIZZA AND A SIDE OF cheesy bread. The cheesy bread is awesome 'cause it comes with two dipping sauces. I can never decide which I like more: ranch or marinara. So I take turns dipping, every other sauce for every other bite, until they're both gone.

Benny comes over late to watch this horror show we like called *Monsters*. Every week, it's a different story. The last one was about a giant spider in a basement shaft who ate people. When I try to make Ford go to bed, he refuses. "I wanna watch too."

"It'll give you nightmares," I say.

Ford shakes his head no. I force him to go to bed anyway. I'm all excited for the show. When the creepy theme song comes on, I hear whimpering and then soft crying. I realize Ford snuck out and is hiding behind the couch, watching.

Benny starts laughing. "Look at the baby cry! Hah!"

For some reason, this really pisses me off. "It's *not* funny!" I say. "He *is* a baby." Then I hit Benny as hard as I can in the arm.

Benny holds his arm like I shot him. Without a word, he storms out of my apartment. Which makes me even more mad. All I wanted to do was watch my show in peace and now everyone is upset.

"Turn off," Ford is crying. "Too scary."

"It isn't real. It's just TV."

Ford is still crying though. I know how it feels to be scared—really scared—of something. And when that something won't go away, it's awful. I don't want Ford to feel like that. No one should have to feel like that.

So I change the channel.

———

ON SUNDAY, FORD AND I ARE IN THE COURTYARD AGAIN. WHEN Benny and Brad come outside, I wave Benny over. "Sorry about last night," I say. He shrugs, but I can tell he's still mad. I get it. I'm that way too.

Brad says, "Come hang with us."

"I have to watch Ford."

"Bring him along," Brad says. "I have to watch this baby too." He points at Benny.

The four of us meet up with some older kids I've never met. Two of them are from the other side of the fence, Liam's neighborhood. The other is named Charlie, who says he's the apartment manager's son. I ask, "Do you live here?"

"Used to. Before I got sent to juvie."

"What's juvie?" I ask.

"Juvenile hall," Charlie snorts, like I'm stupid. "After my folks split, I stole my old man's car. Red-hot Camaro. I was drinking whiskey and beer and crashed the vintage piece into a bank."

"Badass," Brad says.

"Yeah, badass," Benny agrees.

It sounds like a lie to me. If it is true, then Charlie is an idiot. Everyone knows you're not supposed to drink and drive. That's how people get killed. But I don't say that.

"You ever had Jack Daniel's?" Charlie asks.

I don't know what that is. I wonder if it's like a Roy Rogers or a Shirley Temple, you know, a drink with cherries in it. I lie and say, "Sure."

Charlie looks around for adults, then pulls a flask from his jean jacket. He takes a sip, then passes it to the two boys from the nice neighborhood. They drink a little and pass it to Brad. He takes a swig and his face goes all sour.

"Strong, ain't it?" Charlie smirks. "I steal a little bit from my momma's cabinet every day. Refill it with water. She's so drunk all the time she doesn't notice."

Brad hands me the flask. I sniff it. I want to try it, but part of me gets worried I'll pass out like Sam does when he drinks. And I have to watch Ford. "No thanks."

"Don't be a weenie," Charlie says. "Just drink it."

"No," I say. I hate being told what to do. My mom does that plenty.

Charlie insists. He pushes the flask. "Drink it, pussy."

I hate that word. It's one of Sam's favorite nicknames for me. So when Charlie calls me that, it doesn't have the effect he thought it would. I don't feel ashamed or embarrassed like he wants. Instead, it pisses me off.

"Come on. Drink it."

The more he tells me to do it, the less I want to. I repeat, "No."

"You're a pussy," Charlie says. He rears back his shoulders and fists, like he's an ape about to attack. I surprise myself when I don't flinch. Charlie isn't half as big as Sam, and I bet he can't hit nearly as hard.

"I'll drink it," Benny says. He takes the flask and gulps. He starts hacking and coughing and gagging, like he drank gasoline.

Charlie says, "I've got a game we can play." He waves one of the quiet boys over and puts him in a headlock. "Basically, I cut off the oxygen supply until he passes out. Everything turns fuzzy and white. It's like being stoned, but you're only out for a few seconds."

"That sounds dangerous. Can't you die from suffocating?" Benny says. I think the same thing, but I'm glad Benny says it.

"That's part of the fun," Charlie says. On the side of the courtyard, he squeezes his arm around the quiet kid's face until it turns bright red. Quiet kid starts hitting his arm, then scratching at it.

Then his whole body goes slack. Charlie lays him on the ground real gentle. After a minute, he starts slapping his face. For a second, I think the quiet kid is dead.

Panic floods through me. I wonder what we do. Do we call 911? Do we do CPR? I don't know how to, but I know that helps lifeguards. I look around the courtyard, thinking the cops are going to come in through the breezeways and arrest all of us for murder. I think of Ford in juvie, and I feel nauseous.

Suddenly, the quiet kid sits up, coughing for air. As he struggles to shake it off, rubbing his chest, I feel like I can breathe again too.

"Pretty cool, huh?" Charlie says.

"Not really," I say.

Charlie rolls his eyes.

"Me next," Brad says. "Do me."

Brad goes, and then the other quiet kid goes. When it's Benny's turn, he looks scared. I say, "You don't have to."

"Shut up, pussy. We're just having fun," Charlie says.

"Let me try it," Brad says. He locks his arm around Benny's neck. He starts to squeeze, and Benny's face starts to turn red. His freckles seem to glow, making his face look like a giant strawberry. He starts slapping his brother's arm. Benny is shaking his head, and starting to flail. Like he refuses to pass out.

"Let him go, Brad!" I shout.

But Brad is looking to Charlie, who shakes his head no. Brad doesn't let up. Then, Benny punches Brad right in the crotch. They both crash to the ground.

I rush over to Benny. "You OK?"

Benny doesn't say anything. He's trying really hard not to cry.

"Your turn," Charlie says to me. "You're the only one who hasn't gone."

There's no way I'm doing that. So I say, "After you go."

"I already did it today," Charlie says.

"I didn't see your turn. Did any of you?" Everyone shakes their heads. "See?"

"I did do it. Twice."

I ask, "Then why not a third time?"

"I don't need to prove anything to you," Charlie says. "Pussy."

Ford repeats it, only he says, "Poothy!"

"Don't use that word," I say.

"Poothy!" Ford repeats, even louder. Everyone laughs, except me. So Ford keeps saying it, until Charlie gets annoyed.

"This is boring," Charlie says. "Let's do something else. Anyone have any whippits?"

"What's that?" I ask.

"It's when you suck nitrous oxide from a whipped-cream can." Brad says this like everyone learns it in first grade. "It's fun. Makes you feel all warm inside. Anyone have any whipped-cream cans at home?"

Everyone shakes their head, no.

"I know exactly what we can do. It's practically the same thing," Charlie says. "Follow me."

I hate this Charlie kid, but I'm curious. I take Ford's hand and trail behind everyone else. Charlie leads us between some giant hedges and the apartment walls. Several air-conditioner units are humming. Charlie kneels down and screws a cap off one of the tanks. He hunches over, and sucks on it. There's a hissing sound as gas shoots into his mouth.

"Nope, I'm done," I say. "You're an idiot. That stuff is poisonous. Look, it has a poison symbol right there on the can."

Charlie flips me off.

"Benny, come on, let's go," I say.

Benny looks at me, then looks at his brother. I realize it's the same way Ford looks at me, like he needs approval. Brad shrugs. Benny says, "I'm staying."

"Stay if you want. But don't do it. Don't be stupid."

"You're stupid," Charlie says. This time, I flip him off.

I want to get as far away from these idiots as possible. I ask Ford, "Want to go get some ice cream?"

Ford nods, a huge smile on his face. We leave Vista Nueva and walk up the street to the Fast-Mart at the big intersection at LBJ Road. It isn't that far, but Ford's still little so it takes us almost twenty minutes. I make him hold my hand the whole time. The only time I let go is when we're in the store and I have to pay. With the last of the pizza money, I buy us each a chocolate-covered vanilla ice cream on a stick.

We sit outside in the shade of the convenience store. We nibble the cold treats slowly, enjoying every bite. This is a treat. Mom never lets us get stuff like this. I ask my brother, "How is it?"

He nods, melted chocolate smearing the lower half of his face like a painted beard. A man walks by and tips his cap, saying, "Hello."

Ford says, "Poothy."

I snort, but quickly add, "Ford, don't say that." Since I'm half laughing, my brother doesn't take me serious. He keeps saying it. Each time, I laugh harder. When I laugh, he laughs. Finally, I'm laughing so hard, tears stream down my face. When someone else walks by, going into the Fast-Mart, Ford says, "Poothy." The man laughs too.

But then Ford says it to a woman getting her gas. She takes off her sunglasses and glares at us. "Excuse me! What did you say?!"

"Poothy!" Ford says. I'm trying to stop laughing, but I can't.

The woman shakes her keys at us, shouting, "What disgusting, foul language! Where is your mother? I hope she washes your mouth out with soap!!"

Ford gets so scared, he drops his ice cream on the ground. He hides behind me.

"Calm down," I say to the woman. "He's a little kid. He's just playing."

"Well, you're old enough to know better! You need to teach him manners," she shouts. Then she storms inside, and starts yelling at the cashier.

"I in trouble?" Ford asks.

"No. But don't tell Mom, OK?"

"Pomise," Ford says.

While I use the store's water hose to clean Ford's face, sirens blare past us. Two ambulances, a cop car, and a fire truck speed by, lights flashing. I don't think much of it as we start the walk home.

Ford repeats, "*Woo-woo-woo-woo!*"

As we approach the apartment complex, we see the flashing lights. The emergency vehicles are everywhere, with cops telling people to get back. A crowd of our neighbors are standing around, watching. I tug on old Mr. Juarez's sleeve and ask what happened.

"Bunch of stupid kids got high on Freon, from the air-conditioners. Instead of inhaling it, guess some of 'em drank it. Turned blue and green, started puking all over my sidewalk. One of 'em passed out. So I called the cops. Ambulance already took two of 'em to the hospital. Probably saved their damn-fool lives."

I look for Benny. I feel sick to my stomach. I don't care about Charlie. Would serve him right if he got sick. But Benny's just a dumb kid, doing whatever Brad tells him to. I walk around the crowd to the other side, and see Benny and Brad sitting on the back of an ambulance. Benny has chunks of wet puke all down the front of his clothes. Their dad is screaming at them while the paramedic tries to calm him down.

That's when someone grabs me from behind. I'm about to scream till I realize it's Mom. She shakes me so hard, I think my head is going to snap off.

"*WHERE WERE YOU?!*" she shrieks. "*I thought you were dead! Did you and Ford suck that Freon too?!*"

"What? No!" I say, trying to pry myself loose.

Sam grabs me with his giant hands, and shakes me even harder. "T-t-tell the d-d-damn tr-tr-truth! D-d-d-did y-y-y-you and F-F-Ford s-s-s-suck that ch-ch-ch-chemical cr-cr-cr-crap?!"

"Tell us if you did now!" Mom shouts. "It's *poison*. The ambulances are right here. They can take you to the hospital. Tell us, dammit!"

"No! Get off me!" I shout. "Ford and I didn't go anywhere near that stuff. I'm not an idiot! Those kids were doing it, so I took Ford to get ice cream!"

Then Mom and Sam do something weird—they hug me. Like, really hug me. They pick up Ford and hug both of us. They hug us real tight and real hard. This is our first full family hug. I've seen them on TV but never had one. Feels kinda nice, but also kinda alien and real embarrassing 'cause some of the neighbors are watching.

"See?!" Mom shouts at strangers. "I knew *my* son wasn't stupid enough to do that crap!"

Except she didn't know. She thought I had, which is why she and Sam wigged out. I roll my eyes.

We get upstairs and Mom won't shut up about how worried they were. But Sam is still red in the face, so crimson it's like the color of the fire truck outside. His hands are shaking. He turns to me, saying, "G-g-go to your room."

"What? Why?" I ask.

Sam starts to take off his belt, and I already know.

"What are you doing? I didn't do anything wrong! I told you, we didn't do anything!"

"W-w-we tr-trusted you with F-F-Ford. Y-y-you left the ap-apartments," Sam stutters. He grabs me, dragging me toward my room. I snake out of his grip, he grabs me by the shirt. It rips as I try to get away. But he has both hands on me, picking me up and carrying me.

"Mom!" I scream. "Tell him I didn't do anything!"

Mom shakes her head. "Sam's right. We told you not to leave the apartments."

Ford starts crying. He reaches out for me, saying, "No! Leave Rex lone!" Our mom picks him up while he cries and cries and cries, shouting, "Stop!"

"Sh-sh-sh," Mom shushes Ford, like he's going down for a nap. To me, she says, "We told you *not* to leave the apartments. Sam needs to teach you responsibility."

That's when Sam starts lashing me with his belt. My legs, my butt, my back. I try to escape, but there's nowhere to go.

The worst part for me, though, is Ford watching.

Little kids shouldn't have to see stuff like this.

SUPERHEROES

When I grab my lunch tray, I notice. The school cafeteria smells better than usual. I crane my neck to see what it is. Turkey, stuffing, mashed potatoes with gravy, all that sort of stuff. They even have cranberry sauce. It's like paste from a can, not with real berries, which is good. The can stuff is better anyways.

There's a big sign that says THANKSGIVING ALL WEEK. I get real pumped 'cause I love holiday feasts. We never have them at home. Mom says Thanksgiving is a big waste of money. I don't see how, since the whole point is to eat food. Eating food is never a waste of money. Last year, we had microwave TV dinners on Thanksgiving.

My mouth is all watering and my stomach is like growling all fierce as I get my lunch tray loaded up with all the treats. I'm so excited to eat this, I don't even care that I have to say, "Free Lunch" to the cashier.

Ethan waves from our usual table. When I sit down, I wince, scrunching up my whole face.

"You OK?" Ethan asks.

"Yeah, I'm fine," I lie. I don't say the truth—that it hurts anytime I sit 'cause I got whipped so hard.

"What'd you think of the *X-Factor* comics I loaned you?" he asks.

"They're good, but *X-Men* is way better. Though I think I like the *New Mutants* ones the most, 'cause those characters are our age."

"I disagree. *X-Factor* is the best. They're the five original X-Men."

I shrug. "How is it that these heroes get beat up all the time, and in the next issue, they're back for more?" I ask. "You never see them in a hospital or resting in bed with a black eye or in a cast or anything."

"Excellent question," Ethan says. He starts giving his theory.

I keep shifting the way I sit, so the weight is on my legs, not on my bottom cheeks. It's awkward though. No matter how I sit today, I can't get comfortable. I even bunch up my sweatshirt and try to make it a pillow, but it doesn't work.

The food is real good though, so I try to focus on that. When I eat, I like to get a little bit of everything in my mouth. A bite of turkey with mashed potato and gravy and dressing. Then a tiny bit of the cranberry, 'cause there isn't much of it. The cornbread stuffing is my favorite, so I try to leave some of it for last. I like the last bite to be the best bite.

Ethan takes all of his lunch items out of a brown paper bag. Almost every day, he brings his lunch. Usually I'm jealous, 'cause his lunch looks better than mine. Most of the time he brings left-overs, like spaghetti and meatballs, or lasagna. Other days, it's a sandwich, baby carrots, and a bag of potato chips. His stepmom must buy the variety pack, 'cause every day it's a different kind or flavor. Ruffles. Lays. Cheetos. Fritos. Sour cream and onion. BBQ.

Chili cheese. Cool ranch. I love chips. My mom doesn't buy them too often, but Abuela always has them stocked up when I come visit. Then when I leave, she gives them all to me to take home.

"—the other thing I love about the X-Men is that they protect a world that fears and hates them," Ethan continues. "I really wish I had superpowers so I could be a hero. I'd protect all kinds of people. I mean, I guess it'd depend on my power set, but I'd travel the whole planet to help everyone. You know?"

I nod. "That'd be cool."

"If you had superpowers, what would you do?"

Without thinking, I say, "I'd kill people who beat up their kids."

"Whoa," Ethan says, putting his sandwich down. "That's a bit dark, isn't it? Heroes don't kill."

I shrug. "Wolverine does."

"But the X-Men don't approve of it when he does that. Good guys don't kill bad guys."

"Maybe they should," I say. "Bad people deserve to be punished."

"But if the good guys kill, what's the difference between them and the evil people?"

I never thought of it like that. As I'm rolling that idea around in my head, Ethan is looking at me all weird. Like he's trying to read my mind. He asks, "Are you talking about in real life, or comic books?"

"Comic books." I take another bite of my food. Chew. Swallow. I don't look up when I add, "But in real life too."

"Oh. I guess that's fair," Ethan says. "I guess that's why we have police and lawyers. There's a whole system in place. Do bad

things, go to jail. Do really bad things, kill people, and you get a
death sentence."

"Yeah, but sometimes the law isn't enough. Bad guys go to jail,
they get out, then commit crimes again. It happens all the time.
That's why Batman is stupid. He catches bad guys, puts them in
jail, and a few months later, he's chasing them around again. If you
do like Wolverine does, and kill the bad guys, they're done. They
can't hurt people anymore. They got what they deserved."

"I didn't know you were so hardcore," Ethan whispers, almost
to himself. "I guess if you and I were on a team, I'd be Cyclops, and
you'd be Wolverine. I'd play by the rules and you'd do whatever
you want. That's a good dynamic. I'd keep you in check though, so
you don't cross the line."

"You couldn't stop me," I say. I feel myself getting mad. I don't
know if I'm mad at Ethan, or just 'cause.

"Be honest. Would you *really* kill bad guys?" Ethan asks. "Do
you think you could take someone's life?"

As I think about it, I get this sick feeling inside. Like I'm all
alone in the darkness, even though its daytime and I'm surrounded
by people. My face gets all hot, my eyes blur a little. It's like I'm so
mad, I want to cry. I won't cry though. Not in school.

I think about when Sam hits me. When he hits my mom.
I wonder if one day he'll hit Ford. I feel this rage boil up in my gut,
and I question if I could do it.

I want to be able to—to hurt Sam the way he's hurt me and
my mom. And to hurt my mom the way she's hurt me. But I don't
think I could. It makes me ashamed. I feel weak. Maybe Sam is
right. I am a pussy. And a coward.

"Rex?" Ethan asks.

I shake my head. "No. But I wish I could. I know it's wicked and awful and terrible, but the world has so many evil people in it. You ever watch the news? The bad things people do to animals? To kids? To each other? I'm so tired of people getting away with doing bad things. They should be punished.

"I mean, that's what God used to do. People were jerks, so he flooded the whole world, killed off the whole human race except Noah and his family and all those pairs of animals. If I were God, I would punish bad people too. No, wait. You know what? Actually, I'd just make it so that they don't exist in the first place. Snap my fingers, and poof. They're gone. I wonder why God doesn't do that now."

Ethan's eyes get all big. He takes a deep breath. "Man. I wasn't ready for this. This is a heavy philosophical discussion."

"The world sucks," I say. My whole body is tingling, like I wanna fight someone. Or maybe run out of the cafeteria and just keep running forever and never come back.

Ethan is staring at me and I realize my eyes are all welled up with tears, 'cause I'm on the verge of crying. He whispers, "You OK?"

"I don't know," I say, fighting really hard not to cry. I'm embarrassed, waiting for Ethan to make fun of me. But he doesn't. He doesn't say anything, until I catch my breath again.

He says softly, "You might not think I do, but I get it. We all have our demons. But you can't let the dark stuff control you."

I wonder if Ethan has secrets. I doubt it. He may not like his stepmom, but she makes him a brown-bag lunch. I don't think

I can remember my mom ever making a meal, except maybe cereal. Ethan doesn't get it, he doesn't deal with the stuff I do.

But I guess he's still right.

"OK. Maybe I wouldn't kill anybody. But I'd find ways to punish the bad guys, like in ways they couldn't recover. Child molesters, I'd cut off their hands. Then tie them up and hang them on a sign and carve what they did into their foreheads so everyone would know. For people who hit their kids, or beat their wives, I'd break every bone in their hands. Tell them if they do it again, I'd come back and do every bone up to their shoulders."

Ethan slaps the table. "Hot damn! I love it! That's so awesome. Why didn't I think of that? *We* should write a comic book!"

My friend keeps talking about all the awesome adventures we could have as superheroes. All I can think is that maybe I'm not one of the good guys. I may not be capable of killing, but I want to hurt people. Good guys don't think the horrible stuff I do. Maybe I'm not so different from Sam. Maybe I am a bad person.

The thought makes me want to throw up.

Suddenly, I lose my appetite.

TURKEY

Abuela lives three hours away, in Abilene. But she's driving to Birmingham to join us today, for Thanksgiving. From my bedroom, I can see the Vista Nueva parking lot. I stand there, watching, waiting for her Toyota to pull up. When it finally does, I run downstairs to greet her.

We hug for a long time. She smells of Dove bar soap, and her skin is soft, like Kleenex tissue. She kisses me, right on my ear. She does it so hard, my ear pops. It's so weird, but she's been doing it since I was little. Now it makes me laugh.

"How was the drive, Abuela?" I ask.

"Fácil," she says. "Easy. I would make a thousand drives to see you, mi hijo." She kisses my other ear and it pops too.

"Gandma!" Ford squeals, running toward her. She hugs him and kisses his ears too. He squeals and clasps his hands over them. "Don' kiss my ears!"

"Hello, Mother," Mom says with ice in her voice. She does not smile, her arms crossed. She keeps her distance.

"Hello, Luciana," Abuela says. She walks over and hugs my mom. Mom doesn't hug her back.

"Don't just stand there," Mom barks at me. "Get her things and bring them upstairs."

Abuela's smile turns into a thin line. "I will help you."

"Rex has it," Mom snaps. "Let's go upstairs."

Abuela doesn't listen. She comes over and repeats, "I will help you." When she opens the car trunk, it is full of groceries. Some are in bags, some are in boxes.

"What is all that?" Mom groans, her pitch higher than usual. "We can buy our own groceries, Mother. We have money."

I say, "No, we don't."

Mom glares at me. It's her look that says I'll pay for that comment later, after Abuela leaves. I try not to think about it.

"It is just a few things for the boys," Abuela says.

Mom is annoyed. Without a word, she turns and goes back upstairs. I'm already digging through the grocery bags. Variety packs of cereal, chips, and cookies. Fruit roll-ups. Chocolate bars. Granola bars. Loaves of bread, jars of peanut butter and grape jelly. Packets of oatmeal (just add hot water!), canned fruit in light syrup, bags of pretzels, microwave popcorn. Boxes of rice and macaroni and cheese. Cans of vegetables, soup, and SpaghettIOs—my favorite. My mouth waters at the sight of all the future meals and snacks.

It takes four trips to haul everything up to our second-floor apartment and into our small kitchen. As I proudly stack everything on the empty shelves, I announce, "It's like Christmas came early!"

Abuela smiles when I smile. Mom doesn't. Her arms are crossed, and she sways from one foot to the other, like a cobra waiting to strike.

Abuela and Ford bring up some plastic bags from her backseat. She starts handing out the contents, some to Ford, some to me. New shirts, socks, underwear. There are several boxes of shoes. "I did not know your exact shoe size or what you like, so try them on and pick whatever you want to keep. I can take back the rest. I saved the receipts."

"*Mother*," Mom says. It's only one word, but it's loaded with fury.

Abuela forces her smile. "I bought everything at Dyess Air Force Base. Everything is cheap for a military widow. No taxes."

"You're spoiling them," Mom sneers.

"That is what grandmothers do," Abuela says. "Please let me do this."

Sam opens the front door and waves. "I-I-I'm home."

"Don't you dare track those boots in here!" Mom shouts.

"I'm n-n-not." He stands there, trying to pull off the knee-high black rubber boots from his new job. His white uniform is covered in green grass stains and dirt. He reeks of harsh, toxic chemicals, smelling the way a battery tastes when you lick the ends. He does lawn care, working from six in the morning till six at night, Monday through Saturday. All day long he sprays weed killer and fertilizer on people's lawns. It sounds like an easy job, but he says its hard work.

When he finally has his shoes off, he comes inside. "H-h-hello,

G-Gabriela," he says to Abuela. He genuinely smiles and hugs her.
"W-we're s-so glad you c-c-could c-come."

"Gracias. I am happy to be invited," Abuela says.

For dinner, Sam decides to cook his favorite: sausage and
sauerkraut. "I thought cooking was women's work," I say, trying
to use his logic against him.

He snorts, shaking his head. "Th-this is German f-food. *Man's*
f-food, like th-the f-food my ancestors used to eat. W-w-we're
Vikings, right, Ford?" Sam flexes his arm.

"Veekings!" Ford says. He flexes too.

I almost correct Sam, that Vikings were from farther north.
Their mortal enemies, the Saxons, were from Germany. Then
I think better of it.

Mom serves dinner on paper plates. The wet food soaks
straight through, so when I cut the sausage, it tears the plate, and
the juices leak onto the table. Mom shrieks, "You're making a
mess!"

"Well, you shouldn't serve soupy food on paper plates," I say.

"Do you need me to buy you plates, hija?" Abuela asks.

"No, Mother, we have plates," Mom snaps. "But I don't like
having to wash them every time we eat. Paper plates are easier."

"We have a dishwasher," I say. "And using paper plates for
every meal is bad for the environment."

Mom glares at me again. Strike two. I'm not doing it on
purpose, I don't think. But I do feel braver when Abuela is around.
No one will hit me in front of her. They'll wait till she leaves.

I don't like this food, but Abuela gives me a look, saying, "Eat."

She eats every single bite on her plate. She always does. She uses the bread to soak up the last of the meat juices and catch the little pieces of sauerkraut. Like she appreciates every morsel. I know she was poor growing up in Mexico. I wonder if it was hard for her family to get food too.

After dinner, Abuela makes up a bed on the couch. Then, she insists on tucking me in. She closes the door gently and sits down on my sleeping bag with me. "Mijo, do you want me to buy you a bed?"

"No, Mom would get mad," I say. "I'm fine on the floor."

There are tears in Abuela's eyes. She whispers, "You know how much I love you. I wish I could make your problems go away. But your mom—" Her voice trails away.

"I know," I say.

"She is very proud, your mother. Stubborn." She takes a breath, and her lips quiver. "So stupid. Why won't she let me help?"

"I don't know," I say.

"Me either," she says.

There are more tears in Abuela's eyes now, but she smiles anyway. She leans in and hugs me for a long time.

———

FOR THANKSGIVING DAY, THERE'S NO WAY MOM WILL LET US COOK in the house. She insists it will make a mess, and she doesn't want to clean. Instead, we go to Luby's. It's just like a school cafeteria, but for adults, and nicer. All the workers wear maroon aprons and funny chef hats and they say "Yes, ma'am," and "Yes, sir," to everyone, even to me.

First, you get a tray, then silverware wrapped in a cloth napkin. Then you go down this long service line, where they have all kinds of different foods laid out behind glass and hot lamps. If you want roast beef or turkey, they slice it right there, so it's fresh. Or you can get chicken, either fried or grilled. They have all kinds of sides too, including four kinds of corn: on the cob, spicy, regular, or creamed. There's also a bunch of salads, in big bowls, all surrounded by ice, but I never get that. Then they have all kinds of cakes and pies and puddings. It's pretty amazing.

We come whenever Abuela comes to town. Usually, I get the Salisbury steak with cheese and little crumbles of bacon on it. But today, I get turkey and stuffing and all that stuff instead. Abuela speaks Spanish to the Luby's line workers, saying, "¿Le darás más por favor?" I don't know what it means, but they smile and give me an extra scoop of everything I order.

I ask, "Abuela, can I get dessert?"

"Of course." She smiles. "Whatever you want."

"He doesn't need it!" Mom snaps.

"He is a growing boy," Abuela says calmly. "Let him eat."

As soon as we sit down, Ford and I start shoveling food into our mouths. Abuela touches my hand, saying, "Let us pray first."

"Oh, yeah. OK." I put my fork down and swallow what's in my mouth. At home, we never pray before we eat. But with Grandma, she always asks us to. She goes to church every Sunday. Wednesday nights too. Mom rolls her eyes at the request, but Sam seems to enjoy the prayer.

"Dear God, we thank you for this meal that you have provided us. We thank you for each day's blessings and for allowing us to be together on this wonderful day. We ask that you continue being bountiful and giving—" Abuela continues to pray for a long time. My mouth is watering, looking at all the food on the table.

But I'm also thinking, *Why is Abuela thanking God for the food?* She's the one who pays for it. She worked four jobs to save up money and get out of Mexico, and she put herself through college, and now works, like, six jobs. And volunteers too. Then, she gives all her money away to her children and grandchildren. God doesn't do that. *Abuela* does. But she thanks him over and over. I don't understand. I don't think he should get all the credit when she's doing all the hard work.

So when she finishes her prayer, I add, "P.S.: Thanks to Abuela, for everything she does. She does more than anyone I know. Amen."

Abuela smiles and says, "Gracias. Amen."

Mom stares daggers at me, like I said something truly evil.

———

AFTER LUNCH, WE HEAD HOME SO SAM CAN TAKE A NAP. HE SAYS he's tired from working long days all week. Abuela thanks him for driving us to a lovely meal. She can always find something nice to say to people, and she's always real polite.

At our place, Ford sits on Abuela's lap while she reads to him. I sit with them too. It's a dumb baby book, but I follow along anyway. It's nice to sit together, warm. Not like temperature warm, but nice warm. I'm not sure how to explain it. I guess it's like a hug without all the hugging.

Mom watches from the other side of the living room, standing in the corner, staring at me, Ford, and Abuela. Like a tiger watching her prey. Finally, she walks real slow like and sits on the other end of the couch. She doesn't do anything. She doesn't watch TV or read a magazine. She just sits there. Watching us.

I can tell she's mad about something. She's boiling inside. I know a fight is coming, and all the warmth in the room goes away. Like Mom is vacuuming up all the joy. Mom never lets us have a nice day. She always wants to ruin it.

Mom is a bomb, just waiting to go off. It's making me more and more uncomfortable, her watching us like that. I hate waiting for the big explosion, so finally I ask, "What?"

"What?!" she snaps back.

"Why are you staring at us?"

"You just look like you're having so much fun," she growls through clenched teeth.

"We are," I say. "It's nice to act like a family."

"Fine! If she's so amazing, why doesn't she raise you?!" Mom yells.

"Luciana," Abuela says gently.

"I'm serious. I'm here twenty-four hours a day, seven days a week, raising these little brats! But you come around a few times a year, and they think you're a saint! You're so amazing, with all your clothes, and all your food, and all your gifts!"

"Luciana, stop," Abuela says.

"I bet Rex wishes you were his mother!" Mom shouts.

"You know what? You're right! I do! Because she's not a crazy person!" I shout back. As soon as I do, I know I shouldn't have. Strike three.

The bomb goes off. Mom explodes. She leaps off the couch and stomps into the kitchen. She opens the cabinets, pulling all of the new groceries out, throwing them into the trash. Screaming, "We don't need your charity, Mother! We don't need any of it!"

"Mom, stop!" I shout. I try to interfere, but she's a storm. I grab at her hands, trying to pull the food away. Then I start pulling the food out of the trash, putting it back on the shelf, trying to match her pace. She shoves me, pushing me so hard, I fall backward, my head slamming into the wall. The room goes hazy for a minute, but this is nothing. I get up, and again, try to stop Mom.

"This is my house! I'll do what I want!" she wails, pushing me back. "And I don't want her charity. I don't need her help! I don't need anyone's help!"

Ford starts crying.

I don't know how, but Abuela stays very calm. She moves slowly, speaks softly. "Luciana, please. It is just food. I did not mean to upset you."

"Everyone loves you. With your perfect job! And your perfect house! And your perfect money!" Mom bellows. "You're just so perfect!"

"No one is perfect," Abuela says. "I certainly am not."

It isn't enough to throw sealed boxes in the trash can. Mom is ripping open the cereal boxes and the bags inside, spilling the contents everywhere, so she can stomp on it. "I don't want this! This is my house! *Mine!*"

"Stop!" I'm shouting, begging. Every time her foot comes down, I think of the meal she's taking away from me, from Ford. "Stop it! What's wrong with you?!"

"Wh-wh-what the h-hell is g-g-going on?" Sam shouts, annoyed that he's been woken. He stumbles onto the scene, his beer belly hanging over stained white briefs, the only thing he's wearing. He takes one look at Mom and he shakes his head. "Wh-what is this?"

"Mom's gone crazy! She's throwing away all the groceries Abuela brought!" I shout. I can't stop shouting. It's like when Mom goes crazy, so do I. Her insanity is contagious.

Sam yells, "L-L-Luciana, st-st-stop it!"

"No! This is *my* house!" Mom shrieks as she rips open a bag of rice and pours it into the sink. "She can't come in here and buy everyone's love!"

"I said, st-stop it!" Sam growls.

But she doesn't.

Sam grabs her arms, pinning them while she kicks and screams and shouts. When she wiggles a hand loose, she slaps at him. Hard, across the face. He grabs that hand, but the other gets free. She claws at his chest, drawing blood.

Abuela sits down, putting her hand over her mouth. She's trying not to cry. "I am sorry. I will take it back. I will take it all back."

"You *can't* take it back!" Mom screams. "You can't take *any* of it back!"

Sam wraps his arms around Mom from behind, picking her up. She kicks and bucks, so he drags her, thrashing and flailing, to their bedroom. He slams the door shut and locks it. He's shouting, and she's screaming. The walls shake and the floors tremble. Then the familiar sounds of violence start, the fleshy thuds I know too well. Even without seeing, I know the sound of slapping, of punching.

I look at the mess of food crushed all over the kitchenette, crunched into dust on the linoleum. I feel like I've been punched in the stomach. Such a waste.

"Let's go for a walk," I say to Ford and Abuela. They are both in tears. "Come on. Walking outside helps. Trust me."

I lead my grandmother and my brother outside. The skies are blue, the grass is green. There is a cool breeze in the air. Abuela holds my hand but doesn't speak. Ford stops crying when I point out a butterfly.

We leave the apartment complex, and walk to Liam's neighborhood. As we walk, I peer inside people's windows. Families are sitting around a table of food, eating and laughing. Others are still cooking, chatting in the kitchen. Some are finished, or haven't started, and sit on their couches watching football or the parade. Everyone is content. They are happy. Thankful.

Me? I don't have anything to be thankful for.

SPELLING

"*Transform*," Mrs. Winstead says.

That's easy. *Transform*. Like Transformers—the cartoons and toys and the animated movie that was real dark—but without the "*e-r-s*" at the end.

"*Possess*," Mrs. Winstead says.

That's easy too. Bunch of scary movies have that word in their title, like *Possession*. Drop the "*i-o-n*."

I'm in English class, taking a spelling test. I'm not that smart, so I have to study pretty hard. Luckily, I have this thing I do in my head, like a memory thing. Any word the teacher says, I think of a TV show or a movie or a song or a video game that has the same word. Then I know how to spell it.

"*Controversy*."

That one's harder. But it's always in the news.

"*Evolve*."

That word is like *evolution*, which is in about a dozen science-fiction books I've read.

"*Agony*."

That word I know. I don't know how, but I do. It reminds me of home. So I write it fast and try not to think about that stuff.

"*Marvelous*," Mrs. Winstead says.

That one is super easy. Like Marvel Comics. But add an "*o-u-s*."

"*Poverty*." Mrs. Winstead looks at me when she says it. She does that on purpose. I know 'cause she looks right at my shoes. They're too small, and one of them split at the front, so you can see my sock. I curl my toes to hide them.

I had new shoes for almost a whole day, but Mom made Abuela take them back. She made her take everything back. The clothes, the toys for Ford, the books for me. The only thing we got to keep was the food. Sam made my mom keep the food—what was left of it.

But she made Abuela leave. Abuela had to drive home after dark, all three hours by herself, back to Abilene. That night I barely slept. The idea of Abuela having to drive home with a car full of gifts made me so sad I wanted to cry, or hit something. The next few days, I refused to talk to Mom. Not one word.

She didn't care.

The Monday after Thanksgiving, I went back to school and Sam went back to work. When we came home, all the food was gone. Every last Cheerio, vanished. "Don't bother looking for it in the dumpsters either," Mom said with this real gloating smirk. "I drove that crap to another apartment complex to dump it. You'll never find it."

She and Sam got into another huge fight that night. Usually I try to stop it, to calm down the screaming before it turns into hitting. Not this time though. Instead, I took Ford to Benny and Brad's. I thought, *Let them fight.*

I know that makes me a bad person.

But I can't help it.

I'm so sick of living like this—so full of hate.

I hate Sam cause he beats Mom. I hate him even more for beating me. I hate Mom for beating me. And I hate her even more for going crazy all the time. I hate that they don't have money. I hate that they always fight about not having money. I hate that all the kids at my school seem happy all the time. Sometimes I hate the whole world. Sometimes I don't know who to hate. I guess, most of the time, I just hate myself.

"The next word is *Vagabond*."

She probably doesn't think I know the definition, but I do. It's another word for homeless. It may not be a nice place, but I have a roof over my head. I can't see my own face, but I feel it turn red. Mrs. Winstead squints her eyes at me, so I do it back at her.

I don't back down when Mom or Sam glare at me. I'm not going to when some crotchety old Mrs. Winstead does it.

"*Vagabond*," she repeats.

I'm so mad I want to throw my desk at her. I don't though. I write down *vagabond*. I double-check to make sure I spell it exactly right.

"*Savage*."

I don't look up this time. If she's looking at me, I might explode. I try to tell myself that I'm not like Mom, that I'm not a bomb. But I feel like I am.

"Eyes on your own paper, Mr. Ogle," Mrs. Winstead says, poking her finger on my desk.

"I was looking at my own paper," I say.

She clears her throat, adding, "*Loathe.*"

I want to write on my paper: *I know what you're doing.* I wish I could. But I'd probably get in trouble.

The old bat is like a hundred years old. Wears her gray hair up in a big beehive on her head. Wouldn't surprise me if actual bees lived in there. They wouldn't make honey though. They'd make poison.

"*Forsaken,*" she says. She has to be doing this on purpose. She has to. Just to piss me off. "*Forsaken,*" she repeats. "OK. Pencils down. Pass your spelling quizzes up."

She lets the class free read for ten minutes while she grades our papers. The whole time, I'm so mad I can't focus on my book. I read the same paragraph about twenty times before I finally give up.

Mrs. Winstead passes the quizzes back. Her red pen gives me an 85, saying I missed three words. There's no way. I double-check. I triple-check. They're all spelled exactly right. My insides are on fire when the bell rings.

The other kids rush out of class. I stomp straight over to Mrs. Winstead, and slam my quiz down on her desk. "These are right. I made a hundred."

"Clearly you did not," she says.

Without looking, I spell out loud. "Erupt. E-R-U-P-T. Cultivate. C-U-L-T-I-V-A-T-E. Quest. Q-U-E-S-T. See? I know all these in my head. Easy. I'm not stupid."

Mrs. Winstead squints at me. She looks at the paper again. Then says, "Your *u*'s look like *w*'s."

"Jonny *Quest* is a cartoon—" I start to explain.

Mrs. Winstead interrupts, saying, "Cartoons are *not* literature."

"I know that! But I've seen it a hundred times. I wouldn't spell *Quest* with a *w*. I know it's a *u*."

"Fine. I'll give you a 95. Minus five points for bad penmanship."

The hairs on the back of my neck stand up. My fingers curl into fists. But I'm not Sam. I don't solve problems with my fists. Instead, I say, "By the way, your *math* is wrong. You only gave the class nineteen words, when there's supposed to be twenty. You forgot a word. Here, let me give you a recommendation for one."

Instead, of saying it, I write it at the top of my paper in capital letters.

P-R-E-J-U-D-I-C-E.

Without looking at her, I storm out of her classroom. For the first time in days, I can feel a big grin on my face.

———

THE NEXT DAY, MY VICTORY VIBES HAVE VANISHED. I'M ALL nervous when I walk into English. I expect Mrs. Winstead to hand me a detention slip or send me straight to the principal. Instead, she looks down at her desk, embarrassed-like. That confuses me.

When the bell rings, Mrs. Winstead walks to the front of the class, saying, "Everyone, pull out your books. Free reading starts now." Then she walks over to the door, wringing her hands like they're wet, and says, "Mr. Ogle, may I see you in the hallway please?"

A lot of the kids go, "*Oooooh*," and some go, "You're in trouble."

Some just snicker or whisper. Now I'm pretty sure Mrs. Winstead is going to give me detention. Or maybe I'll be suspended. Or worse, maybe a police officer is waiting outside the classroom. I can't go to jail for being rude to a teacher, can I? It sounds crazy, but I'm sweating like it's real possible.

When I walk out of the classroom, the hallway is all empty. I don't know if I've ever seen it like this, all silent, without students. It looks all wrong, which makes me even more nervous.

Mrs. Winstead closes the door so it's just me and her. I open my mouth to apologize, thinking maybe it's not too late to save myself, but the English teacher cuts me off. "I'm not a racist," she says. "I am a devout Christian and attend church every Sunday. I have an open heart to all people, blacks, Asians, even Hispanics, like you—"

I am about to explain I'm only half, but she cuts me off.

"I am a good person." She pauses. "But you were right. I have shown . . . prejudice toward you. And I owe you an apology."

"No, you don't," I whisper, still worried about detention.

"Yes. Yes, I do," she says. "I am sorry."

I don't know what to say. Mrs. Winstead has always looked so tough and mean—until now. She's never looked so old before. And shaky, almost fragile, like Abuela did the other day. I feel real horrible about the whole thing, but also glad she's apologizing.

For the first time, she looks at me. Right in the eyes. It's kinda uncomfortable, 'cause I've never looked at a teacher like this for this long.

She asks, "Do you forgive me?"

I shake my head. "Yeah. Sure."

I surprise myself when I say it, 'cause I realize I mean it. I guess if I can forgive Mom and Sam for all the things they do, it's a whole lot easier to forgive other people for the real small stuff.

GLASS EYE

I n industrial shop, we are cutting wood to make birdhouses. Mr. Lopez says we can take them home and hang them in our trees in our yard. I don't have a yard. But I decide I can give it to Abuela for Christmas.

This kid, Jake Russo, runs across the shop. He play-punches Kent Graham in the arm, then pushes me. I'm sliding a piece of wood under a giant saw when he does this, and I nearly lose a finger. I'm about to freak out when Jake says, "You'll never guess what I just spent my lunch money on!"

"What?" Kent says.

"Guess!"

I say, "You pushed me when I was using the saw, you idiot."

"Lunch?" Kent guesses again.

"Nope. Guess again."

"A skateboard?" Kent guesses.

"No. Guess again."

I say, "We're done guessing. Just tell us."

Jake Russo says, "I paid Tommy Garcia to take out his eyeball."

"Seriously?" I take off the protective glasses and look past the electric saw machines and wood planks for Tommy. He's in our grade but he's a foot taller and two years older. He's failed twice. He wears a jean jacket with the sleeves cut off, and his hair is long, down to his waist, like a rock star.

Kent asks, "What do you mean, he took out his eye? Like it fell out?"

"No, he has a *glass* eye. I gave him two dollars to take it out."

I ask, "Was there blood?"

"No, but it was so gross—and *sooo* awesome!"

"You just went up to him and asked him to take out his eye? How did you know he had a glass eye? I didn't."

"I heard about it from Jenny Patel in first period. She said he did it last week on a dare. I wanted to see. I asked if he'd show me and he asked how much money I had. It was the best two dollars I've ever spent. You have to see it!"

I don't know why, but I really want to.

It's like when all my friends see some new scary movie, and I haven't. Everyone keeps talking about it, and I'm all annoyed 'cause I want to see stuff too. Only this time, only one person has seen the scary movie, so I have a chance to see it early, be one of the cool kids who sees it first. Only, I don't have two dollars. Though I do have four quarters.

Every day, when I come home from school, I do this thing where I go through the apartment laundry room and check all the coin returns. People are always forgetting to do that, so I get the left-behind quarters. I also check the pay phone. Sometimes there're coins in it too. I planned on using the change to get a bag of chips or a Kit-Kat from the new vending machines at school, but I'd rather see Tommy's glass eye.

"I have a dollar," I say.

"I have a dollar too," Kent adds. "Want to go together?"

"Yes!" I don't even hesitate. In my head, I keep imagining what it must look like. If there's goo or slime or like stringy eye snot or maybe some blood. I get goose bumps thinking about it.

"When should we do it?" Kent asks.

"Now," I say.

We walk over together, but we're both going real slow. There's sawdust and woodchips all over the ground. Mr. Lopez is too busy reading a car magazine to notice. I'm getting all nervous. I think maybe part of me is freaked out, or maybe worried that Tommy will get mad and cut us in half with one of the table saws. I mean, I know that's stupid and he won't, but that's the kinda stuff that runs through my head.

Anyways, Kent and I both get to Tommy and just stand there.

After a minute, Tommy looks up from sweeping his area and says, "What?"

Kent looks at his hands and doesn't say anything. I step like one inch forward and try to talk. "Um, we were, uh, wondering, if . . . we could, I don't know, maybe . . ."

"Spit it out," Tommy says.

"You know . . . see your eye . . . like Jake Russo."

Tommy stares at me for what feels like more than a full minute. Then he rolls his eyes, only one doesn't go all the way up. "You got two bucks?"

We hand him the money.

"It's two dollars *each*," Tommy says.

"Oh. Uh, that's all we got."

Tommy is annoyed. Looks at us like he's going to punch us both in the face. He could too. He's kinda a giant compared to us. Finally, he sighs. "Fine."

He waves us into the corner. He checks over my shoulder to make sure Mr. Lopez isn't watching. He isn't. So Tommy reaches up, digs his fingers into his eye socket. He fishes around for a few seconds. Then with the sound of a tiny suction, he pulls out the glass eye.

It's not the whole eyeball like I thought. It's just the front part. But I'm not staring at the glass eye—I'm staring at the socket, where the eye was. It's pink and fleshy and hollow.

"Can I hold it?" Kent asks.

"Hell no," Tommy says. He turns around and struggles to put it back in. We don't wait. We run off.

At lunch, I sat down next to Ethan and say, "You'll never guess what I saw!" When I tell him, Ethan loses it. He keeps asking me all these gory questions about every little detail. He thinks it's sick and awesome too, just like me.

The next day, I see Tommy being led into the vice principal's office. I wonder if he got sent in for taking out his eye. It seems like one of those weird things that you can't really get in trouble for, since you aren't hurting anybody, but that teachers will get real annoyed about anyway.

When I see him next in industrial shop, I ask, "Did you get in trouble?"

Tommy says, "Yeah, bunch of preppies ratted me out. Thought

I was gonna get suspended or detention. Vice principal probably woulda but I told her I was just doing it for lunch money. Can't get mad if I'm trying to feed myself."

"Is that true?" I ask. "Were you doing it for lunch money?"

"Nah," he laughs. "I get my lunch for free."

He said it. Just like that. No shame. No embarrassment. Just, wham!, here's the truth.

I can't explain it, but suddenly I feel like Tommy and I are closer. Like we're family. Or at least friends. I mean, I knew someone else had to get a free lunch, but I didn't know who. I always wanted to look in the red folder to see, but felt like that's an invasion of privacy or something. Anyway, I must have some ridiculous grin on my face 'cause Tommy says, "What? Why you looking at me like that?"

"I'm—I'm in the Free Lunch Program too," I say. "You want to, I don't know, maybe sit together sometime?"

Tommy laughs real hard at that. He says, "Nah, dude. I don't sit with losers."

HOUSE

After school, I walk up the stairs to the apartment. I fish my keys out of my backpack, but I don't need them.

The door is wide open. Busted out with a hammer, the lock hangs there like a dead metal animal. Pieces of a sheet of a paper are taped to the door, but someone's ripped it off so nothing's left but the corners.

My first thought is, *We've been robbed again*. The first time someone broke into our place was pretty horrible. They stole my first Walkman and all my cassette tapes and our cat got out and never came back. The last time we got robbed, joke was on the robbers. We didn't have anything to steal, so they broke through the window for nothing. The weird part is you get robbed more living in bad neighborhoods than if you live in nice ones. I'd think bad folks would wanna steal nicer stuff.

But now, as I peer inside my apartment, there's no thieves. Just Mom packing. She's doing it real fast. We don't own much, but what we do have is tossed into cardboard boxes in the center of the living room. I don't understand what's happening. The air escapes from my lungs. "What's going on?!"

"What's it look like, stupid? We're moving," Mom says.

I flash back to fourth grade, when I changed schools five times in less than four months 'cause we kept moving while Mom and Sam looked for work. Having to start over with new friends and new teachers and new classes at a new school in a new town is hard enough. It's even worse when your parents pick you up in the middle of the day in a packed truck, and you don't get to say goodbye to anyone. One day you have a new friend, and the next you'll never see them again.

"No!" I shout. I grab a box and dump it out on the floor. "No way. Uh-uh. I like Birmingham. I like my friends. I'm not going anywhere! I'm not moving again!"

Mom rolls her eyes. "Quit being so dramatic. We're not leaving Birmingham. We're moving across town, walking distance from your school. You won't even have to ride the bus anymore."

"Wait, really?" I think of the neighborhood I see every day on the bus ride to school. It's all pretty houses on tree-lined streets. The houses aren't huge, maybe only three or four are two stories high. But the places are real cute, painted nice pastels. A lot of them have white picket fences. One has this big red rose garden and a stone fountain with a mermaid in it. Even the ones that aren't that nice are a lot nicer than Vista Nueva.

I've never lived in a house before. Even if it needs work, that's OK. I can paint the house, the insides and the outside. Sam can do the lawn with the chemicals from his job. Mom is good at cleaning, so she can make the inside real nice.

We'd have a little yard for Ford to play in. Maybe we could get a dog. I could have friends over and not feel embarrassed about the roaches or the creepy neighbors. Maybe we'd even get furniture.

"Are we really moving to a new house?" I ask.

"It's not new, but it'll be new for us."

"Used is fine," I say. I'm so giddy, I want to know every detail. "When did this happen? Why didn't you tell me?"

"'Cause it's none of your business," Mom says. "We needed a change. Change is good, right?"

I nod. I run into my room and start packing, the whole time daydreaming about our new house. It only takes me twenty minutes to pack everything I own. After, I help Mom finish packing everything else. We take it all downstairs and load it into the back of Sam's work truck. That's the good part of not having furniture—moving is super easy.

I run over and say bye to Benny and Brad. I make sure to write down their phone number so I can call them. We can still hang out since Sam and their dad are drinking buddies. I consider running over to Liam's to tell him the news, but Mom says we don't have time. Liam and I never hang out anymore anyway. Maybe things'll be different when I'm in a house. We can practice football in the backyard. Or the front yard.

I feel all light and glowy and warm. I can't name the feeling for a while, and then I realize I'm just really happy. Not just for me, but for my whole family too. I bet even Mom will be happier. I'm excited for something new.

As we eat McDonald's for dinner, I'm giggling at everything. "Do Ford and I have our own rooms?" I ask.

"No," Mom says. "It's a two-bedroom, one bath."

That sounds like our apartment, but that's fine. A house is better than an apartment, 'cause it means you have more money. Plus, we'll have a yard. "Can I paint my room?"

"I don't care," Mom says. "As long as you pay for the paint."

"Cool!" I say. I ask Ford, "What color do you want our room to be?"

He says, "Bwack!"

"Black? Like a cave? That might be cool."

"You're not painting your room black," Mom says.

"Pink?" Ford asks.

"No," Sam grumbles. "P-p-pink is a g-g-girl's color."

I realize that Sam's been quiet this whole time. Mom is grumpy too, but she's always grumpy.

"Why aren't the two of you more excited?" I ask. "Aren't you excited?"

Mom shrugs.

I consider asking where they got the money for a house, but I know better than to talk about money in public. It's a touchy subject. We're obviously renting, not buying. Renting is cheaper than buying.

"So tomorrow, when we move in, the first thing I'll want to do is—" Mom starts, but I interrupt her.

"Tomorrow? We're not going tonight?"

"No. Tomorrow."

I ask, "Where are we sleeping tonight?"

"In the car and the truck," Mom says like it's nothing.

"What?!" I squeal, completely confused.

"It's just for one night," Mom says.

"Why can't we just spend the night at our new place?"

"It won't be ready until tomorrow at noon."

"Can't we get a motel?"

"No. That's a waste of money to just go sleep. We spent all of our cash on the new place anyway. Don't be such a baby about tonight. It's like camping."

"You hate camping! And it's December! It's freezing outside!"

"You aren't sleeping outside. You're sleeping in your sleeping bag inside the car," she says.

My voice squeaks when I ask, "Where am I supposed to shower before school?"

"You can skip a shower for one day. It's not going to kill you if you stink a little."

"I don't want to stink!"

Sam slaps his fries off the table. They fly, scattering all across the floor. Other families look over at us. Sam growls, "Sh-sh-shut u-u-up! B-b-both of y-y-you! N-not another w-word."

I'm so caught up in my own thoughts, I don't realize till now that Sam isn't just quiet, he's pissed off. He won't make eye contact with me. Is he mad cause we're sleeping in our vehicles, or is it something else?

Now I'm wondering about the broken lock and the taped note on the door that I never saw.

Maybe moving so suddenly wasn't our choice.

Maybe we had to leave.

Quietly, I ask, "Did we get kicked out of Vista Nueva?"

Sam throws the rest of his burger at me, pegging me in the

chest with it. Ketchup and mustard splash my shirt. He shouts, "*G-g-god-d-d-dammit!*" He storms out to his truck. Outside the window, I can see him kicking and hitting it. Mom glares at me. "Look what you did. Are you happy?"

I'm not happy, but I also don't see the big deal. So we got kicked out? At least we're moving into a new (used) house. That's good, right?

That night, Sam sleeps in the cab of his work truck. Mom and Ford sleep in there too. I sleep in Mom's car, alone, in the driver's seat. The passenger seat is piled with boxes, and there's so much in the backseat, I can't recline. With the steering wheel in the way, I can't get comfortable. There's also a streetlamp just above, glaring off the windshield. I toss and turn all night, can't sleep. When I finally get up, I have this horrible crick in my neck.

We go back to McDonald's for breakfast. I really like their breakfast menu, especially the hash browns. I try to focus on how crunchy and greasy-good those are, and think of how tonight I'll be sleeping in a new room in a new house. I wonder if the window will face the front or the back or the side. Honestly, I don't care.

The plan is to go sign the papers and get the keys. Then we can go see our new place. After I have a key and see where we live, I can walk to school. I'm excited that I'm so close to home now.

After breakfast, we drive the tree-lined streets of our new neighborhood. I keep trying to guess which house is ours. We drive past the ones I hope for. Finally, we pass the school, still driving. I ask, "Where are we going?"

"There." Mom points. As we drive into the parking lot, my dreams shatter like a glass bottle thrown against the wall.

We don't pull into the driveway of a house. We pull into the lot of a black-and-white brick apartment complex. It's on the far side of the middle school's football fields, just before the train tracks. On the other side, you can see an old trailer park and a junkyard where cars go to die.

This all feels wrong. Like I've been tricked. I've never noticed this dump 'cause the bus route drives by the houses, not this way. Everything feels confused. Wrong. "You said we were moving into a new *house!*"

"I never said that." Mom sneers. "You said that."

"Why didn't you correct me?"

"House, apartment, it's all the same."

"No, it's not!" I shout.

Driving through the lot, some elderly people are milling about all slow, like zombies, with their walkers or canes. I don't see any kids around. There's no pool. The park is all dead grass, and puddles of mud. There are some swings and climbing sets, all made from old tires. Vista Nueva was a dump, but it was a dump with a pool. It was way nicer than this. This isn't a step up. This is a step down.

I find myself already missing the cockroaches.

The apartment complex manager's office looks like an abandoned church, and has the name *Royce Court* scrawled across in an old country-western font. Ford and I follow Mom and Sam inside. While they're signing the contracts and getting keys, I read papers taped to the fake-wood-panel walls.

Something called the Department of Housing and Urban Development (HUD) sponsors the complex. It allows "reduced rent for low-income families." That means it's public housing. That means the government is helping to pay for our place—the same way they're paying for my lunch.

My stomach turns upside down, and the hash browns slosh around. I feel sick. Pacing doesn't help, so I sit. I cross my arms, but my legs won't be still. I'm shaking. I stare daggers into Mom's back, wishing they were real blades. She ignores me while she and Sam sign the forms. My heart slams inside my chest. Just across the street is the football field, where I can't play football. It'll be a daily reminder of all the things I can't have. What if Liam or Todd—or worse, Zach or Derek—see me walking home over here? They'll tell everyone. Everyone will know that I live like this.

The manager hands the keys to Sam and Mom. He shakes their hands politely. They pick up Ford and walk outside, nodding for me to follow as an afterthought.

We barely make it to the parking lot when I can't hold it in any longer. I shout real loud, "I'm not taking another step until you explain this to me!"

"Explain what?" Mom says.

"Why is the government paying our rent?" I shriek.

"You wouldn't understand," Mom says.

"So help me understand! You're not old. You're not sick. You're not disabled. Sam has a job. And you could get a job if you really wanted. You won't let Abuela buy us groceries, so why are we letting someone else pay our rent?"

"It's not someone else, it's the government. That's their job!" Mom shouts back at me.

"It's the government's job to take care of people who *can* take care of themselves?!"

"*We* CAN'T *take care of ourselves!*" Mom screams at the top of her lungs. "*You think we want to be here? You think Sam and I enjoy moving to this place? Do you?!*"

People are watching. I realize I started this fight, I started shouting, making a scene in public. Just like Mom does. The thing I hate so much, I'm doing now.

"*You don't understand anything. You're just a kid!*" she screams.

"*I'm not just a kid!*" I roar back, unable to stop myself. "*I'm more of an adult than you. I balance your checkbook, remember?*"

"*Then you know all of our money is going to bill collectors for credit-card accounts and old loans. Sam may have a job now, but we're in the negative. We're drowning in debt!*"

The words hit me like an eighteen-wheeler. How did I not realize this? Every month, I watch Mom write the checks. Every month, I double-check her math to make sure every penny is accounted for. Every month, I noticed the money was negative. But I didn't know what that meant. I didn't see the big picture.

I'm ashamed for being so stupid. Ashamed for not understanding why we were always paying late fees and overdraft charges. Ashamed for never thinking of it from Mom's point of view. Or Sam's. Of course they don't want to be here either. Did some part of me think they did?

I feel horrible and nauseous. But at the same time, furious. My heart is beating so hard I hear it throbbing in my ears. The floodgates are open, and I can't stop myself. It's like I'm out of my body, and my body is screaming. All the blood in my body rushes into my face as I scream as hard as I can: "*THIS IS YOUR FAULT! I HATE THIS PLACE! AND I HATE YOU!*"

I see Mom rear back, like a baseball player in slow motion. I don't think to get out of the way, 'cause it happens too fast. Mom slaps me so hard that my left ear explodes in pain. It rings, and keeps ringing.

My brain hurts, like it got hit too. Everything feels shocked, like the time I stuck a paper clip in an electric socket just to see.

Suddenly I'm dizzy, I fall sideways, onto the ground.

Mom is screaming at me, but I can't hear anything from the left side. I can read her lips though. She's saying she hates me too. She tells me to go to school, to get out of her sight. She looks like a rabid pit bull as she comes at me, barking and gnashing her teeth. Sam holds her back. He is dragging her away from me. He takes Ford and they leave.

I lie there for a long time, not moving.

On the ground, inches from my eye, I see a line of ants marching along. They look busy. All working together, not apart. I bet they never fight. In this moment, more than anything, I wish I were an ant.

PAWNSHOP

——

I am full of dread going home these days. Mom and I haven't spoken in a week. When we're both home, she just glares at me, like I'm her worst enemy. Like she hates me. Which is fine, 'cause I hate her too.

She's a grenade, my mom, but you can't see the pin, if it's in or out. So Sam, Ford, and I sit around, waiting for her to explode. I'm never relaxed. Never calm. Or happy. I'm always on edge.

Like when we're eating, I wait for her to stab me with a fork. When she's ironing, I'm worried she's going to hit me over the head with it. When she's driving, I expect her to drive off the road on purpose 'cause our car doesn't have airbags.

That's why yesterday, I stood outside my front door for ten minutes, scared to go inside.

That's why today, I've been standing here for almost fifteen, my hand on the doorknob. I take a deep breath, then open it.

Inside, Sam is unplugging the TV. He picks up the TV and moves it onto the floor. I ask, "What are you doing?"

His eyes are angry and embarrassed at the same time. He

doesn't give me an answer. I notice a big box filled with stuff from around the apartment. Inside are the toaster, the stereo, a bunch of Sam's music collection, my Sony boom box. It's black and can play two cassette tapes at the same time. It was a Christmas gift from my real dad. I growl, "What're you doing?"

"A-a-ask your m-m-mother."

My muscles tighten as I fill up with rage. I can't stop myself. I stomp to the bathroom, where Mom is blow-drying her hair. I rip the cord from the wall, roaring out, "What are you doing with all our things?! What are you doing with the TV?!"

She shouts, "No one watches it anyway."

"We all watch it! Every day!"

"Well, you like reading books too. So just do that!"

"And my boom box?!"

Ford is sitting on the floor. He slams a plastic *T. rex* into his favorite fire truck-toy. He says, "Pont chop."

"Pont chop?" I adjust Ford's way of speaking. "Do you mean *pawnshop*?"

Ford nods. "Pont chop!"

I turn toward Mom. "Why are you pawning our stuff?"

"Exactly!" Mom half snorts, half laughs. "It's just *stuff*. No one really owns anything. It's all just junk."

"Well, this time it's *my* junk!"

Mom grabs an inch of my flesh, twisting it. The way she pinches like this, it leaves purple and blue star-shaped bruises that are sore for days. I get these all the time. But this time, she's merciless and doesn't let go. I scream in agony, my legs buckling under me until I'm on my knees.

"You think I want to pawn our stuff? I don't! But sometimes we have to. That's how we keep the lights on, that's how we eat!" Mom uses her thigh to kick me over. She plugs her hair dryer back in.

I'm not letting her get the last word. I snatch the dryer from her hand, yank the cord out of the wall, walk into the living room, and throw it into the box with the rest of the things.

"If Sam and I have to do without, then so do you!"

"Fine!" Mom screams. "You'll be lucky if we get six dollars for it. I don't care! You don't know how it feels to . . . You know what? *You* go to the pawnshop this time. I'm not going. *You* see how it feels to beg for scraps. Go on. Sam, take him with you!"

"L-L-Luciana—" Sam starts.

"No!" she screams. "Take him. He's never been. He hasn't seen how hard it is to give away your own stuff. Take him! Let him learn what it feels like firsthand!" She picks up the cardboard box, shoves it into my arms. She storms into her bedroom, slamming the door shut so hard the whole apartment shakes.

"C-c-come on," Sam says.

———

SAM DOESN'T SAY ANYTHING AS HE DRIVES. NEITHER DO I.

On our way to the pawnshop, we pass all these really fancy shops and restaurants. These are the kinds of places where people buy gold watches and real paintings and jewelry and expensive clothes. One place sells these little crystal figurines for, like, hundreds of dollars apiece. One of the restaurants is this fish place, where the cheapest dish is, like, thirty dollars, and that's just for a salad. We've never eaten there.

Mom and Sam have pawned stuff before. The TV and stereo they've pawned a bunch of times. Usually just for a few days. But they've never pawned the toaster or anything of mine. I guess that's why I got so mad. But I'm also worried. Can Mom and Sam not pay their bills at all? Are we going to have to leave Birmingham? Where would we go after government-subsidized housing? Are we going to be homeless, live under a bridge and ask for change on the side of the highway? I've seen people do that.

I fill up with worry. Are we going to starve? Are we going to die?

I try to think of other things I can pawn, but I barely own anything except books, and those you can only sell to used-book stores for like a quarter. Fifty cents if it's a hardcover. Maybe a dollar if it looks like new and you're lucky.

When we pull up to the store, Sam doesn't look at me. Almost like he can't. He gets the TV out of the backseat. I get the box with the other stuff. I follow him inside. There's an old golden bell on the door that chimes when we walk in. After the first door, there's a second door, so we're trapped in a cage in between.

An old man comes out from a fluorescent-lit back room. He watches us through an inch of scratched-up glass, a protective-barrier with a sticker that says, BULLETPROOF. The wall is reinforced with metal bars. They remind me of a jail cell.

The pawnbroker presses a buzzer and the second door opens.

When the man sees our stuff, he motions us over to a counter. All around, there's rows and rows of junk for sale. Jewelry and rings and watches all locked up behind more thick glass. TVs, stereos, electronics are safe behind red metal cages. There's all these other things too, like fur coats and porcelain cats and seashells and pewter statues of cowboys. The wall is all clocks and neon-light beer signs. There are bookshelves, but no books. Just more junk.

I wonder who would buy some of this crap. A lot of it is dirty or stained or broken. Though I guess some of it is kinda cool. Like a wooden box all carved with naked women. A handheld black-and-white TV. A bunch of hunting knives, some cool ninja throwing stars. At the back of the store, there's a whole shelf filled with boxes full of all kinds of toys. I dig through, wondering what they have. There's a few really cool action figures, but most of them are missing an arm or a leg. I wonder who owned these toys, and how they got here.

This real sick feeling fills my stomach, and I feel like crying. I don't. But I feel like it. Then I get really mad at myself for being such a wuss.

Sam is stuttering worse than usual. I pretend I'm not listening, but I am.

"H-h-how m-m-much f-f-for all o-of it?"

"Eighty-five," the old man says. I try to do the math in my head. The TV is old, but alone, it's worth twice that.

"Ei-ei-eighty-f-five? C-c-come on, m-m-man. It's Chr-Chr-Christmas this m-month. M-m-make it a h-hundred and tw-twenty."

"Eighty-five," the old man repeats.

"S-s-screw th-that," Sam says. He grabs the TV, ready to leave.

The pawnshop owner says, "Reynolds Pawn closed last month. I'm the only shop in town." Sam hesitates, then puts the TV back.

"G-g-give me a h-h-hundred and t-t-ten."

"I'll give you ninety-five," the pawn man says. "Final offer."

Sam's knuckles turn white as he grips the counter. "F-f-fine."

The old man writes an invoice, tears the yellow copy from the white-and-pink ones. He gives the duplicate to Sam. He counts out ninety-five dollars in cash from his register, recounts it, then gives it to Sam through the slot in the bulletproof glass.

The way pawning works is this: You take stuff to a pawnshop. You sell it to them, but like, for temporary. The pawnshop gives you some money. Not a lot, but it's cash, so you can spend it right away for milk or gas or whatever. Then, you have thirty days to go buy your stuff back. If you don't though, they own it. Then they can sell it to whoever for more money. So if you come up with the money after the thirty days, you have to buy it back at a higher price. It's not a good system, but it's the only one there is, I guess.

When we get back in the truck, Sam is quiet. He stares outside, his face turning more and more red. He peels out of the parking lot a lot faster than he should, and we nearly hit a car. At the next red light, he hits the steering wheel, slamming his fists down again and again and again. He doesn't care that it's honking the horn and people are staring.

I shrink down in my seat, trying to make myself smaller, hoping Sam'll forget I'm there. I wonder if he'll turn on me next. Like when Mom pulls the car over and hits me for no reason.

But Sam stops on his own. He shakes his head, hiding his eyes behind his hands. "I-I-I'm s-s-sorry. I-I-I'm s-s-sorry you h-h-have to s-s-see that. S-s-see th-this."

"See what?"

"Me. B-b-begging. C-c-crying," Sam sniffs. "I-I'll g-get y-your b-b-boom b-box b-back. E-e-even if I have to w-work m-more hours. I will. I pr-pr-promise."

He's never promised me anything before. It catches me off guard. I say, "It's OK." Then I add, "It's just a boombox. I don't need it anyways."

We sit in silence until the light turns green. Then we drive home.

SPILLED MILK

Ford asks, "Choc-lit milk?"

"What do you say?" I ask.

"Pease!"

"That's right. Good job." My brother loves chocolate milk. So do I. Especially the kind you have to make yourself. Mom won't buy us the powder or the syrup, but Abuela does. Mom didn't get it in the Thanksgiving purge. 'Cause I hid it behind a pipe. Today, I squirt the last of it into a glass. We have just enough syrup for one.

"Can we share it?" I ask.

Ford nods. There's a lot I don't like about having a little brother: Cleaning his messes. Bathing him. Feeding him. Babysitting all the time. But it's cool when he's nice, 'cause I guess that means I'm doing a good job. Plus, he can be pretty funny.

I let Ford have the first sip of brown milk. He gulps these little-brother-sized swallows. When he's done, milk coats the area above his lip. I say, "Nice mustache!"

He says, "Stash?"

I drink some the way he did, so I have a milk mustache too. I point out our reflections in the oven window. We both laugh.

I hand the glass back to him. He's sipping slowly when it slips out of his hand. Milk splashes all over the floor. He looks up at me with these big wet eyes—scared. That was the last of the chocolate syrup, and I start to get real mad, but only for like half a second, 'cause I see Ford is about to cry.

I remind myself he's just a kid. He didn't do it on purpose. I say, "It's fine, Ford. It's OK. Let's just clean it up before—"

Mom rounds the corner and sees the mess everywhere. She screams like one of us cut off our fingers or something.

"It's fine, Mom. I'll clean it up."

Mom snatches up Ford, raising her hand to slap him. I grab her hand. "Stop! It was an accident."

"It was the last of the milk!" Mom shrieks.

"We'll get more."

"*How? With what money?!*" she cries. She starts pulling at her own hair, shrieking and moaning. She hits the cabinets with her fists. Then she slides down against the wall, sinking onto the kitchen floor into the spilled milk. Her hands are covered in it when she brings them up to her face. The milk runs down her arms and drips onto her legs, soaking into her shorts.

She just sits there, sobbing, crying for a long time.

That's when I realize.

She's broken.

I don't know if she was born this way, or if something broke her along the way. Maybe being poor broke her. But she isn't well. And she can't get well as long as this is her life.

As much as I want to, I can't hate her. She's my mom. My only mom. I crawl over, into the milk, and hold her. She's moaning now, like some ghost is trying to escape her from deep down inside. The sound makes every part of me feel loaded with guilt, so heavy I could drown in it.

I have to stop fighting her. I have to try to help her.

I just wish I knew how.

APOLOGIES

"I'm sorry," I say.

"For what? What'd you do now?" Mom asks. She's barely talked to me for days. Instead of being mad about it, I keep reminding myself: *Be nice to her, be nice to her, be nice to her.*

"I don't know. For everything," I say. "I know I'm not easy."

"You're telling me," she says. But Mom eyes me closer, waiting for something. "What's the catch? You apologizing because you want something?"

I shake my head. "Nope. I just want to say, I know it must be hard. Dealing with what you deal with. Adult stuff, I mean. Paying bills. Trying to find work. All that stuff."

She can't tell if I'm sincere. But I am. Some part of her knows. She softens a little. But just a little.

There's this part of me, way deep down inside, it's like the little kid I used to be. That part wants to break down, crying and begging, to say I'm sorry for everything. Take the blame for all the bad things. The fighting. The money. The move. Because I just want her to hug me and say she loves me.

But there's another part of me, I guess the part of me from right now, the older me, that refuses to do that. 'Cause I'm not sorry for everything. 'Cause it's not all my fault, and I won't say it is, 'cause that's a lie. I won't take responsibility for the things I didn't do. For her hitting me. Or for Sam hitting me. Or for her fighting with Sam. That stuff isn't my fault. I'm sorry that stuff happens, but I didn't do it. And I won't say I'm sorry for it. But I am sorry about everything else. So that's what I try to say.

"I know I have a temper—" I say slowly. Slowly, 'cause I'm trying to think about what I say before I say it. I want to say, *a temper I learned from you*. But I don't. 'Cause that won't help things. "—and I'm sorry for yelling at you—" I bite my lip this time 'cause I want to say, *even though you always yell first*. "I want to be better. I want to help around here."

Mom's eyes narrow, trying to figure me out. "Good, it's about time you apologized," she says in a nasty tone. But then she softens a little more. Adding, "I'm sorry too. I know this life isn't easy."

"It's not your fault," I say on reflex. I'm not sure if I mean it, but I think it's what she wants to hear.

Maybe what she *needs* to hear.

And I'm right. 'Cause her eyes get real wet, and she's about to cry.

She sniffs and says, "It's really hard. Being poor in this country is like—like starving at an all-you-can-eat buffet. You can see all of this food piled high, but you can't have any of it. It's just out of reach. Like everything else. Jobs. Houses. The things you see in TV commercials. It's all a pipe dream for people like us. It's all window-shopping. The grocery stores, the malls, the car lots everywhere. It's all luxury, and people don't realize how lucky they are if they can afford any of it. We know, because we *can't* have any of it. No matter how hard we work, we'll never have money like the people at the top. We work just as hard as they do. Harder sometimes. But we'll never make the money they make. The system is broke. It's just—it's not fair."

Usually when I say that—it's not fair—Mom says, *Life's not fair.* I don't say that though. I just nod.

"I want to work," she whispers. "I do. It's easy to get a job when you have a job. But the opposite is true too. When you don't have a job, no one wants to hire you. No one wants to take a chance."

"Someone will," I say.

"Who?"

"I don't know. Someone," I say. I offer a little smile.

Mom smiles back. She hugs me.

I know it's not a lot, but it's a start.

SATURDAY

O n Friday, out of the blue, Liam asks me if I want to come
over. "It's been forever. Wanna hang out?"

"OK," I say.

"We can bike around. Like old times."

"I moved. I live on the other side of town now."

"Oh," he says.

"It's fine. I'll be there."

"Cool. See you tomorrow."

On Saturday morning it takes me an hour to walk from Slate
Road to Glendale Avenue. When I get there, Liam is shooting
hoops in the driveway of his two-story house. All sweaty, he asks,
"What took you so long?"

"It's a long walk."

"You walked?"

I shrug. I don't say my mom wouldn't drive me 'cause gas is
expensive.

"You hungry? Let's eat before we bike."

Inside, his mom is making pancakes, eggs, bacon, and fresh

fruit. When she sees me, she runs over and gives me this big warm hug. "Rex, it's been forever! How are you? Oh lord, please pardon my appearance, I'm a mess!"

She's not though. Her hair is perfect, and she's wearing a red holiday sweater, pearl earrings, and a matching pearl necklace. The only thing messy about her is the pancake batter on her hands and apron.

"Liam told me you're not playing football. Good for you. Ever since he started, his grades have been abysmal. I'm tempted to make him quit the team."

"Mom! Stop talking. He's my friend, not yours!" Liam groans.

His mom giggles, then pretends to zip her lips. She hugs me again, and whispers, "It's so good seeing you. Come over again soon. Help yourself to anything in the house."

I load up my plate with a little bit of everything. Liam's mom always makes food just right: the pancakes are the size of silver dollars, the eggs are soft-scrambled, the bacon crispy. She even cut up the best fruits: strawberries, honeydew, and pineapple. When I finish, I get seconds. Liam ignores all the food she made, and instead heats up a Pop-Tart.

After breakfast, we run up to his room so he can grab his bike lock. The house is huge. They have three bedrooms, three bathrooms, an office, an attic, a two-car garage, and a small pool in the back. To me, it seems like a lot of rooms for three people. But I wish I had that.

Liam has two bikes. He loans me one so we can ride around. I follow him to Birmingham Lake. We skip rocks in the water and talk about school and movies and things we used to do in fifth grade. I don't ask about football. It'll remind me of the fun I'm missing. And I don't like being jealous.

When we're riding home, we stop at the Fast-Mart. "I'm thirsty," Liam says. "Want something?"

I'm super thirsty, but I don't have any money. I shake my head no. We go inside the store, and Liam grabs a soda from the fridge. He opens it and starts drinking before he's paid for it. I could never do that, 'cause cashiers would probably call the cops.

He grabs a Gatorade and a bag of chips, tossing each to me. "Carry this, will ya?"

A woman comes in to pay for her gas. Liam looks over his shoulder to make sure the cashier is busy. Then he slips four candy bars into his pocket. He says to me, "Come on, grab something."

I shake my head no.

Liam's dad is a lawyer. If he gets caught, he'll just get grounded. If I get caught, I'll go to jail for the rest of my life.

Liam shrugs. "Suit yourself." He slips a pack of Starburst into his other pocket. Then he walks to the counter, looks the man in the eyes, and smiles real charming-like. Which he is. Everyone likes Liam. Which is probably why he can get away with anything.

He puts the empty Coke can on the counter and burps real loud. "Excuse me." He laughs as he grabs the chips and Gatorade and puts them on the counter. He pulls out a small roll of cash. Mostly fives and tens. He pays for his stuff and winks, saying, "Have an awesome day, dudester."

We're about to walk out when the cashier says to me, "Hey! You not buying anything?"

"No."

"Let me see your pockets," the cashier snaps.

Real annoyed, I lift my shirt and pat myself down. There's nothing in my pockets. Not a single penny. The cashier gives me the stink eye anyways.

When we come out of the Fast-Mart, Liam starts laughing so hard he's crying. "That. Was. *Priceless!*"

"I'm glad you think it's funny."

"It is! I rob the guy blind, and he's staring at you the whole time. We should go to a jewelry store together."

"No, thanks," I say. I'm real irritated for a bunch of reasons. For one, if Liam had got caught, I probably would have gotten in trouble too. Second, I hate that cashiers always think I'm trying to steal something. It makes me so mad. And third, third is the part I just don't get. So I ask. "Why do you do it? You have money. A lot of it. So why? Why risk getting in trouble?"

Liam shrugs. "I dunno. Because I can."

On my long walk home, I think real hard about that. Maybe it's a good thing Liam and I aren't friends anymore. When we were kids, doing dumb stuff was fun. But now I'm getting older. I can get in real trouble. That'll just make things worse. Not just for me, for everyone, like Sam and Mom and Ford.

I know I thought Ethan was a total weirdo when I met him, but suddenly I'm real glad he's my friend. He would never steal something just 'cause. Ethan's a good person. I kinda hope that if I hang around him long enough, I'll be a good person too.

CHOPSTICKS

When I come out of my bedroom, Mom screams, "Rex!" She charges toward me like a bull. I cover my head, caving against the doorframe, bracing myself.

She doesn't hit me though. Instead, she hugs me, squeezing me until I can't breathe. She yells, "I got it! I got the job!" She jumps up and down. She's smiling. An actual, bright, wide, white smile. "I got it! I got it!"

She wraps her arms around me again. It feels bizarre, claustrophobic. It's not that it isn't nice. It is nice, I guess, just . . . unfamiliar.

I ask, "Where?"

"Birmingham's newest restaurant: Mandarin Garden. Rex, this is a game-changer. This restaurant is gor-geous! It's just off the highway in the center of town, so the place will be packed night and day. I'm so excited. I'm going to make so much money! We'll be *rich*!"

Rich seems like a bit of a stretch. But I don't say that. I smile and give her a hug. I ask, "Can we eat there?"

"That's the best part. I get one free meal a day, and any food left over at the end of the night. You can eat there on opening night. They told the whole staff to invite their families. And it's half-off!"

That night, I dream of running on top of giant egg rolls, swimming in steaming egg-drop soup, and battling a giant dragon. He burns off one of my legs, but underneath is a chopstick. I don't get the meaning, if there is one, but I wake up feeling hungry. By the time Friday rolls around, my mouth won't stop watering.

Even Ford is excited. Over and over he asks, "I use stop-chicks?"

"*Chop-sticks*," I correct him.

"That what I said. Stop-chicks!"

Sam gets home an hour earlier than usual. He stinks of weed killer and fertilizer fumes, from the toxins he spent all day spraying on lawns. Thirty minutes later, he emerges from the bathroom a new man. He puts on the button-up shirt he saves for special occasions and church with his mother. His hair is combed and parted, and he smells of cologne. He even shaved.

He asks, "Y y you guys ready to st stuff your faces?"

Ford and I shout, "YES!"

We pull off the highway when we see the sign. MANDARIN GARDEN. FAMILY-STYLE CHINESE EATERY. NOW OPEN!!

The building looks like it was made in China and brought here just for us. Its base is brown brick and black trim. Its windows are bordered by deep red tile and gold detailing. The sloped roofs above shine golden in the setting sun. Large crimson doors are guarded by two giant stone lions. I put my hand in one's mouth and say, "Ford, help! The lion is eating me!"

We all laugh. Ford climbs up, puts his hand in the lion's mouth and says, "Is eating me too!" Usually I'm annoyed when Ford copies me. But tonight, we're all in a good mood.

Inside, the restaurant feels even more authentic. Dragon murals are painted above on the ceilings. The furniture is black with red leather. Gold detailing covers the walls, showing tigers and warriors doing battle.

"Welcome to Mandarin Garden," says the hostess in a thick accent. "Three for dinner?"

"Can we sit in Luciana's section?" I request.

Mom sees us and rushes over. She hugs me and Ford tight, and kisses Sam on the mouth. She introduces us to the restaurant owners, then leads us to her section. She gives us large black menus with golden tassels. "It's so fancy, isn't it?" she whispers to us. "Everything on the menu is in English *and* Chinese."

I try to figure out the alphabet so I can write in Chinese, but I give up so I can read our place settings—which explain the Chinese Zodiac. I really wanna be a Tiger or a Dragon, but my birth year makes me a Horse.

I read my horoscope out loud, "Popular and attractive to the opposite sex. You are often ostentatious and impatient. You need people. Marry a Tiger or Dog early, but never a Rat."

Ford looks confused. He asks, "Marry a dog? But that's a pet!"

When Mom returns with appetizers, we forget about the Zodiac. "This is egg-drop soup, wanton soup, egg rolls with sweet-and-sour dipping sauce, fried shrimp, and Crab Rangoon."

"What's crab ragu?" I ask.

"Rangoon. Deep-fried dumplings with crab, garlic, and cream cheese inside."

"Gross."

"Try it," Mom says. Her gentle grin persuades me to take a bite. As the warm insides of the Rangoon splash onto my tongue, I'm in heaven.

"It's so good!"

"See?" Mom grins. She holds Sam's hand and tells him about her favorite items on the menu. In her black skirt, ironed white shirt, and black apron, Mom is the happiest I've seen her in a very long time. It's like she won the lottery. I try to recall the last time she smiled this much, and I can't.

When she gets another table, Sam slaps her on the butt, saying, "G-g-get to w-w-work, h-hot mama."

Mom giggles. I scrunch my face and say, "Ew! Gross!"

Every time Mom walks by, Ford goes, "Hot mama!" We all laugh.

Ford, Sam, and I talk about our day as we devour the appetizers. Sam asks about school. I talk mostly about art class. Ford tells us about his favorite new cartoon. Sam tells us about work, how he stepped in dog crap, and tracked it into this lady's house on accident, and how she clutched her pearls and almost fainted. I laugh so hard, soy sauce comes out of my nose. That makes all of us laugh even harder. It's weird that I live with Sam but we haven't talked in a long time. I forgot how funny he is when he tells stories.

Mom returns with huge bowls of steaming white rice and platters of lemon chicken, sweet-and-sour pork, pepper steak, General Tso's chicken, and the house special: Mandarin Garden Chicken—fried nuggets in a sweet garlic sauce. I want to try everything. The citrus lemon chicken explodes in my mouth, better than anything

I've ever eaten. That is, until I try the fried nuggets. They're like Chick-fil-A, only better.

We all agree to try to use the chopsticks. Sam gives up after a couple of tries. Ford doesn't, and keeps flinging food all over the table. I laugh until Sam grumbles to stop wasting food. I keep trying, but I can't get any rice in my mouth. I'm too hungry to wait. So I give up and switch to a fork instead.

We eat and eat and eat until we can't eat another bite. I feel sick, but good sick 'cause I'm so full. Even my brain feels all floaty. Mom sits down in the booth, hugging me from the side. She kisses my forehead like she does Ford. She asks, "What'd you think?"

"Oh my God, it's so good," I say. "Can we eat here every night?"

Mom giggles again. "Well, not every night. Maybe once a month. But I can bring home takeout. How does that sound?"

Ford and I high-five each other.

"Oh, I almost forgot!" she runs off, quickly returning with a small golden plate with fortune cookies.

We open them one at a time. Sam goes first. "*L-l-land is al-always on the m-m-mind of a flying bird.* What d-d-does that m-mean?"

Mom reads hers. "*Your shoes will make you happy today.*" Sam and I laugh, but Mom says, "No, it's true! These new work shoes are great for being on my feet all day!"

Ford gives me his fortune so I can read it. "*You will marry your one true love—and soon!*"

Ford's eyes get big, then he says, "Hot mama!" We all laugh. Sam and I roar till tears stream down our cheeks. Mom turns red from trying not to laugh in front of her new bosses.

Finally, I crack mine open and pull out the tiny rectangle of white paper. I read aloud: *"Great wealth is coming your way."*

Pure warmth rushes through my body. "Mom, it's just like you said. You were right."

Mom squeezes my hand and gives me another hug. I could get used to this.

The busboy takes our plates away, returning with our leftovers in small white takeout boxes. Each has a little wire handle and red Chinese temples printed on the sides. The owner, an older woman, gives me more fortune cookies and an extra pair of chopsticks. She insists that I learn to use them before I come back.

Mom walks us outside. She smooches Ford's cheeks, four kisses on each one. She kisses Sam on the lips and hugs him. Then she hugs me again. I don't say it, but I like my new working mom.

"Rex, you should take some of the leftovers to school tomorrow," she says.

"Really?" I ask.

She nods. It's such a great idea. Kids bring sandwiches or pasta or salads. No one ever comes to school with Chinese takeout. It'll be so cool. It's a free lunch without the part where I have to say it out loud.

Before we leave, I run over and hug Mom again. This time, I hold on for a long time.

CHRISTMAS TREE

The best part of the holidays is being out of school for two weeks. On the last day before break, nothing really gets done. The teachers are counting the minutes too. Except Mrs. Winstead. She gives us a pop quiz.

She grades my vocabulary quiz like everyone else. I make a 100. I missed one (*aplomb*, which means being cool when you're actually stressed-out). But I got the bonus word (*lexicon*, which is another word for vocabulary).

At lunch, I'm excited. Even though I have to say, "Free lunch," the cafeteria has turkey and dressing again. Just like Thanksgiving.

When I sit down with Ethan, he asks, "Are you going anywhere?"

"Nope," I say. "You?"

"Colorado with my family, to some ski resort."

"Sounds fun," I say.

"Not really. Traveling with my family is the worst. My dad says flying is too expensive, so we have to drive there. Everyone screams at each other on the car ride. By the time we get there, no one wants to talk to anybody else. We usually spend the first two days in total silence."

I'm surprised. "Your family fights?"

"Every family fights," Ethan says.

I don't say it, but I think, *Your family doesn't fight like my family.*

"You're lucky," Ethan says. "I'd rather stay home. You get to watch TV, sleep in your own bed. I always get stuck sharing a hotel room with my sisters. So gross."

"Wanna trade places?"

"So you can sleep next to my sisters?!" Ethan throws a potato chip at me. I try to catch it in my mouth, but it bounces off my cheek.

"No. I just think vacations are fun." Though the only vacations I go on are to see my abuela or my real dad. I'm not sure if family trips even count.

"Oh, before I forget . . ." Ethan reaches into his backpack. He pulls out a thin rectangle wrapped in red-and-green shiny paper.

"What's this?"

"Are you an alien or something?" Ethan laughs. "It's a Christmas present. Or Hanukkah if you're Jewish. Are you Jewish?"

"I'm not anything," I say. I tear open the wrapping paper. Inside are a bunch of *X-Men* comics, including a special double-sized *New Mutants* issue I wanted. I flip through the pages, staring at the bright colors and the extraordinary art. It takes me a full minute before it dawns on me. "I don't have anything for you."

Embarrassed, I avoid Ethan's eyes.

Ethan shrugs. "That's OK. I'm glad we sit together at lunch. You're really cool. You're my best friend, you know."

I don't know what to say. It's weird to hear Ethan just say what he feels. Before, when I used to call Liam my best friend, Zach made fun of me, said I was gay. But Ethan doesn't think like that.

I say, "You're my best friend too."

Ethan says he doesn't care about a present, and he's telling the truth. Still, I feel this big wave of guilt, like I should have thought of him too. I decide, over the break, I'll make a comic about him. I can write it and draw it, with him as the hero. 'Cause he kind of is—a hero, I mean.

When the final bell of the day rings, I take my time. I always sorta linger in Mrs. McCallister's art class. Taking an extra five or ten minutes to finish whatever art project I'm working on. Then, all slow, I walk to my locker. No rush. I do this 'cause buses pick up behind the school, and I don't want anyone to see me walk to Royce Court.

If I walk slow enough, most of the buses are gone by the time I get outside. It only takes me five minutes to walk from the school to my front door. I know it's silly or stupid or whatever, but I still don't want anyone to know where I live. I can help Mom and Sam by being nicer at home, but I can still be embarrassed about being poor. I mean, I think every kid is embarrassed about something. This is mine.

When I get home, the apartment smells of Windex and lemon Pledge. Mom wears dishwashing gloves and is scrubbing down our television. I say, "You got our TV back!"

"I got paid today!" Mom says. "I even got us a VCR so we can watch movies!" I get excited. I've always wanted to rent movies and watch them at home, like other kids.

Mom keeps spraying and scrubbing. It's her little ritual. After any of our things come home from the pawnshop, Mom spends an hour cleaning them. She hates germs. Plus, I kinda think she loves to clean. We don't have a lot of stuff, but she always makes sure everything is spotless. Heck, she even vacuums every single day.

After the cleaning, I plug the TV in and set up the antenna. I hook up the VCR and make sure it works. Mom is scrubbing the toaster when I remember. "Mom, where's my boombox?"

"About that, honey . . ." Her voice trails off. "There was a mistake at the pawnshop. They accidentally sold your boombox."

My voice cracks when I say, "What?!"

"We'll make it up to you, OK?"

"My dad bought that for me."

"Maybe he can buy you another one," she says.

I can tell she feels bad. And even though I'm feeling crazy and angry, I take this real deep breath. When she tries to hug me, instead of pulling away, I let her hug me. Then I hug her back.

"It's OK," I say.

"What do I always say?" Mom says. "Everything in this life is temporary. So appreciate what you have while you have it."

I nod. It's a dumb saying, but I know what she means.

Trying to be a better person is really hard. I don't know why, but it's real hard to not get so upset. Maybe that's just how I'm built.

I mean, the things in our home have always gone away. Sometimes they go for a short while, and sometimes they never come back. Usually it's Sam's or Mom's stuff though. I guess this is the first time something of mine went and didn't return.

Maybe it's about my dad too. I only see him once a year. When I go, he takes me to the mall and buys me clothes and new shoes. That's not 'cause he's being nice. Him and my stepmom are just embarrassed to be seen in public with me in my normal clothes. The stuff I really want, he never gets me. He says things like, "Aren't you too old for toys?" or "I doubt you're going to read that whole book," or "When I was your age, only girls wore necklaces." But when I asked for the boombox, he bought it for me, so it kinda means a lot.

Now it's gone. The one nice thing my dad did for me. I take a deep breath and try to forget about it. After all, he's the one who left me a long time ago.

Mom disappears in the kitchen and returns with a box. "I got those Ding Dongs you like. The chocolate ones wrapped in foil."

"You did? Can I have two?"

She laughs. "No. But you can have one now, and one after dinner."

I don't know if it's the sugar or the chocolate or the cream filling, but the miniature cake makes me feel better.

———

MOM, SAM, FORD, AND I SIT ON THE COUCH WATCHING TV together. Around the holidays, they always play the same movies. Some of them are real dumb, but I love the one with the kid who wants the BB gun. That's the one we watch. We all laugh, and talk about our favorite parts during the commercials.

The next morning, Sam surprises us and says, "C-come on. We're g-going for a drive."

"Where?" Mom asks.

"Y-you'll s-see."

The four of us drive to Colleyville. On the way, Sam farts. It makes the whole car smell like something died. Ford and I scream and gag. "What is wrong with you?!" Mom shouts. She rolls down the window even though it's freezing out, saying, "Better that we freeze to death than smell your garbage farts."

We're all laughing.

I think we're going to KMart until Sam takes a right, instead of a left, off the highway. We pull into a dirt lot filled with cars and people and Christmas trees. When Sam opens the door, a wave of fresh pine tickles my nose.

"No. Nuh-uh. Absolutely not," Mom says. She crosses her arms, refusing to get out of the car. "Trees are a waste of money."

"I d-don't care," Sam says. "I'm G-German. G-Germans invented Chr-Christmas trees. This year I w-want one. The whole h-house will sm-smell like p-pine."

Mom shakes her head. "Who will take care of it? Who will water it and clean up the needles, and make sure Ford doesn't get electrocuted? Me, that's who!"

"Sh-shush, woman." Sam smiles, kissing her on the cheek. "I'll take c-care of everything."

We used to have a plastic tree. One you pulled out of a box and put together. But one year it didn't come back from the pawnshop.

I've never had a real live tree before. At first, I don't see what the big deal is. But after walking around row after row of firs and spruces and pines, I witness other families doing what we're doing—talking about the trees' smells and shapes, and if it'll fit in the car or through the door at home, and if it's too tall. Suddenly, I realize, we're acting just like everyone else. No, not acting. We *are* like everyone else.

It almost feels like I won a big contest.

My body warms, like I just drank a quart of hot cocoa. I get it now. There's something magical about real trees. Already, I want to do this every year.

I run after Ford and Sam, trying to vote for the tree I like best.

"I still think it's a waste of money," Mom repeats. She won't uncross her arms. Sam is trying to get her to sing along to the holiday music playing from the speakers, but her mood won't budge. He pokes her, saying, "Ch-cheer up. Where's your Chr-Christmas spirit?"

"I don't have any," she says.

He pokes me. "You w-want a tr-tree, right?"

I nod yes. "They smell amazing. Will our whole apartment really smell like this?"

"Yup," Sam says.

"Not with your farts," Mom groans.

Ford and I laugh. Sam points at me and says, "P-p-pull my finger."

"No way, Jose!" I say.

"No way, Jose!" Ford repeats.

"C-come on! For Santa," Sam says. "P-pull it."

I pull it and Sam farts. At the end of the butt trumpet comes a wet sound. Sam's face goes white.

"What's wrong?" Mom asks.

Without a word, Sam turns around and crab-walks toward the highway. "Sam, what's wrong?" Mom calls out after him. We watch as he looks both ways, then runs across the highway and disappears inside the Arby's. Through the windows, we see him run into the bathroom.

"Do you think he's OK?" I ask.

"I think he . . . you know . . . had an accident," Mom says.

"What do you mean?"

She looks around, to make sure no one can hear. "I think he crapped himself."

Ford and I stare at each other. We burst into laughter. Ford laughs, "Daddy poop in pants! Daddy poop in pants!"

"It's not funny!" Mom says—but even she can't hold back a giggle.

Twenty minutes later, Sam returns. "N-n-not a w-w-word," he says. He buys a tree, ties it up, and secures it to the top of the car. We all get in. Mom laughs first. Then Ford and I do too.

"Daddy poop in pants!" Ford says.

Even Sam starts laughing.

<hr />

CHRISTMAS MORNING, FORD JUMPS RIGHT ON MY HEAD. "WAKE up. Santa came!" he shouts with glee. "Santa brought presents!"

I'm too old to believe in Santa, but I pretend along for my little brother. "He did? Let's go see!"

In the living room, there are fourteen presents under the tree. They are wrapped in newspaper and foil. Ford and I pick up each box and give it a tiny shake, trying to guess what's inside. We don't open anything though. We wait until Mom and Sam wake up so we don't get in trouble. Then we have to wait some more. They won't let us open anything until they've had coffee.

I divide the gifts. There's one for the whole family, two for Mom, two for Sam, eight for Ford, and one for me. I check under the tree again, but that's it. Just the one.

For a minute, I'm about to get real upset . . .

Then I think of Abuela growing up in Mexico. And the homeless people who ask for change on the side of the road. I think about how we were homeless for one night, and that was awful. But now we have a roof over our head. And Sam and Mom never let us starve, even if we have to do without TV or a toaster for a little while. Mom didn't sign me up for the Free Lunch Program to punish me. She did it so I could have food.

Maybe Mom wasn't so wrong when she called me a brat. I mean, she wasn't totally right either, but still. Things aren't as black and white as I always thought. Maybe some things are gray, somewhere in between.

I look at my present, and I swallow my anger down. I'm still sad, but I let myself be a little sad. 'Cause I know lots of rich kids who get loads of gifts for the holidays. This Jewish kid in my computer science class was bragging, saying his religion has Hanukkah, and he gets presents every day for, like, a whole week.

I may not have a million presents, but I have one.

And one is better than none.

Who cares? It's all just stuff, right?

I force a smile. Then I focus on Ford, 'cause he's smiling ear to ear as he tears through the wrapping paper on his gift.

He opens the biggest one first, the one for the whole family. It's from Abuela. She sent a giant box full of summer sausages, fancy cheeses, crackers, mints, and stuff. There's even chocolate-covered pretzels, my favorite.

Mom opens her presents. She gets a bracelet from Sam, and a ceramic bowl that I made in art class.

Sam opens his. Mom got him a carton of menthol cigarettes with a fancy new Zippo lighter. I made him this wooden box in industrial shop class.

When it's his turn again, Ford rips open his presents, tossing newspaper and foil everywhere. From me, he gets a fire truck with flashing red lights and a working ladder. Mom and Sam get him a giant yellow dump truck. From Santa, he gets building blocks, some clothes, and a book.

When I pick up my one present, I'm not sure what to expect. The box is the size of a shoe, but it's really light. I give it a shake, and hear the slightest flutter. I have no idea what it could be. Maybe it's something really amazing. I tear off the paper, then pull the tape off the box's edges. Inside, it's a check addressed to me, from my dad. Not Sam, but my real dad. In the "Memo" section, it says, "Buy something fun for yourself!" The check is for fifty dollars.

"It came with the child support," Mom says. "I thought it'd be more fun to open if it was wrapped up." She steps over Ford's pile of presents and grabs my stocking from where it's tacked into the wall. She pulls a little box out of it and hands it to me.

"What's this?"

"Open it."

I do, and it's a check from Mom. "It's for fifty-*one* bucks." Mom laughs, "I had to give you more than your dad. And I promise, the check won't bounce. We actually have money in our account. You can check the math."

I hug Mom. She hugs me back and plants a big kiss on my forehead. She whispers, "I know it's not a lot, but money is still tight. I'm proud of you for being so mature and understanding."

Later, I'm looking at Mom, sitting in Sam's lap, watching Ford while he plays. Ford is pushing the fire truck saying, "Woo-woo-woo-woo!"

Ford crawls into my lap and hugs me. His little arms around my neck, he says, "Thank you for my fire truck." Only he does that thing where he pronounces *tr* like an *f*. I can't help but laugh.

That's when Sam says, "Rex, you m-m-missed something. B-back there, b-behind the tr-tree." Just like in the *Christmas Story* movie they show on TV.

I get up, and look. Sam says, "No, to the l-left. B-behind the TV c-c-cabinet."

Mom looks as confused as me. "Sam, what is it?"

Sure enough, tucked behind the cabinet and the wall is a box wrapped in newspaper. I look all over the box. "It doesn't say who it's for."

"It's f-f-for you," Sam says. "B-b-but you h-h-have to sh-share with your brother, OK?"

I pull off the newspaper. It's a brand-new Nintendo system. It's not even used. It's new. My legs feel like they're going to crumble beneath me. I've wanted one forever. All the kids at school have one. The game console comes with a controller, a gun, and two games: Super Mario Bros. and Duck Hunt. I can't help myself. I squeal and run over to Sam and hug him. And I mean it. I run to hug my mom, but she's as surprised as me.

"Sam—" she starts.

He cuts her off. Calmly, he says, "It's d-done. I thr-threw away the r-receipt. We l-lost his b-b-boombox. It's only f-f-fair."

Mom looks pissed for a second. Sam says, "Let the k-kids have this. We b-both have j-jobs now. We're g-going to be f-fine."

For once, Mom lets it go. Mostly. I can still see it in her eyes that she's annoyed. But she doesn't say or do anything. Not for the whole day.

As holidays go, this is the best I've ever had.

NEW YEAR

As he drives, Sam flicks a menthol cigarette onto his lips, then lights it. He turns the radio dial to a classic-rock station and starts to sing along. It's funny, I've never noticed before, but Sam doesn't stutter when he sings.

Usually, I hate this kinda music. But I don't say anything. Sam is driving me to spend New Year's Eve with Ethan, so I don't care what he listens to.

The windows are down, and the diesel engine growls and rumbles when we stop at the red lights. My nose burns from the lawn chemicals. The back of the truck is two giant tanks, their sides dotted with hoses and metal boxes of tools. The cab of the truck is littered with empty McDonald's bags, stepped-on paper cups, and cigarette butts. Sam pushes the stick shift into gear, and the vehicle lurches forward, weed killer sloshing in the giant tanks behind us.

I've never been to Ethan's, so I don't know what to expect. So when we turn into Ethan's neighborhood, I can't believe how big the houses are. They're all two stories. Some have little waterfalls in the front yards, or metal gates like something from a movie. I double-check the address as the truck pulls up in front of Ethan's house.

"Wow," I whisper to myself. It's practically a mansion.

"Thanks for the ride," I say to Sam. But when I open the door to hop out, Sam grabs my arm.

"H-h-hold up. Th-this is a pr-pretty big lawn. D-d-does your friend t-take care of it, or his d-d-dad?"

I don't have time to answer before Ethan's front door opens. He and his dad walk out. I expected Sam to drop me off and leave. Instead, he hops out of the truck and walks around to this side. He shakes Ethan's dad's hand. "S-s-say, d-do you already have a lawn c-care sp-sp-specialist?"

All the differences between Ethan and me are right there in my face. Ethan's dad wears loafers, a button-up shirt, and a tie. His smile has straight teeth. A nice new car is parked in the driveway. By my side, Sam wears shoes covered in mud and a grass-stained work polo. He smokes a cigarette as he stutters through semi-yellow teeth. His company truck is at our back. I feel this big ball of shame well up inside of me.

Ethan grabs my backpack. "Come on. Let the adults talk."

He drags me inside. The front room is two stories tall and has a curling stairway. Gold-framed pictures of his family hang perfectly on the walls. There are no stains on the carpet, or on the white furniture. Everything has its place, but nothing is overcrowded. Fresh flowers in vases are everywhere. His stepmom leans over the railing from their upstairs TV room and gives a friendly wave. She is wearing a skirt, a pretty blouse, and a gold necklace. She wears lipstick and her hair is done. "You must be Rex. Welcome! If you want anything to eat or drink, help yourself."

"Thanks."

"This way," Ethan says. He signals to go right, into a giant space with vaulted ceilings and a huge window looking out at the front yard. There's a set of bunk beds against the far wall, comic-book posters everywhere, and a huge bookshelf filled with books. He even has a computer on a desk in the corner.

"I'm sorry about that," I say, nodding out the window where Sam is still talking to Ethan's dad.

"About what?"

"My stepdad. Trying to sell your dad lawn care."

Ethan shrugs. "So?"

"It's embarrassing."

"My dad is an accountant. That's embarrassing."

"You don't get it."

"Explain it to me then," Ethan says.

I don't know how to tell him how poor I am. How we live in government-subsidized housing, or how I get free lunch. Instead of saying anything, I stare at his floor.

Ethan pats me on the back. "You do realize *every* kid is embarrassed of their parents, right?"

"Yeah, but—"

Ethan cuts me off. "But what? You think your embarrassment is worse than mine? No offense, but you're not that special. You're just like everyone else. You have issues with your stepdad? So what? I have issues with my stepmom. Welcome to the human race."

"She's so nice though," I say.

"To your face," Ethan says. He closes his bedroom door. "Trust me. She's a nightmare. She definitely doesn't like me."

"Really?"

"Really. She hates my real mom, and by extension, me. The whole holiday ski trip, she was nagging. *'Ethan, don't put your elbows on the table. Ethan, tuck in your shirt. Ethan, we're on a ski trip, can't you put that book down for two seconds? Ethan, why can't you smile more?'* It's exhausting."

"I kinda thought you had a perfect life," I admit. "I mean, you dress nice, and have tons of comics, and you always have homemade lunches at school. I figured your parents must care if they make those for you."

"Ha!" Ethan roars. "I make my own lunch!"

"You do?"

"Yeah, you dope. You shouldn't assume things. And come on, no one has a perfect life. There's no such thing as 'perfect.' It's just an idea."

"I never thought of it like that," I say, really thinking about what that means.

"OK, enough serious talk," Ethan says. "Let's read some comics."

Then I remember what I brought. I pull it out of my backpack and give it to Ethan. He asks, "What's this?"

"Your Christmas present. Sorry it's late. But it's your own book, with you as the hero in it. I wrote the story and typed it up on my neighbor's typewriter. There's a bunch of mistakes, so just ignore the crossed-out words."

"Wait. You made this?"

"It's only ten pages," I explain. "I was going to make you a comic, but I'm not a very good drawer."

"Illustrator," Ethan corrects me, but not in a mean way. "I don't think 'drawer' is a word. Unless you're talking about a desk drawer. Or underpants, but that's plural. Drawers. Never mind."

"I wasn't going to give it to you, but . . ." My voice trails off. I don't want to admit it, that I didn't have any money. But Ethan got me something and I had to get him something. So I made this. Instead, I say, "It's kinda dumb. If you don't like it, that's OK."

"It's not OK," Ethan says. "Dude, it's *amazing*!"

"Come on, it's not that great," I say.

Ethan looks me in the eye. "Yes, it is. This is the best present I've ever gotten."

I look around his room. He has a trunk full of comics and cool posters. He has a TV, a stereo with a CD changer, even a telescope. He probably gets all kinds of cool presents. I say, "Yeah, right."

"I'm serious. What you made—*this*—this is a real gift. It's not thoughtless. Don't put yourself down. What you made is amazing. I love it. Thank you."

"But I didn't spend any money on it."

"Money isn't everything," Ethan says. "Trust me. My family has money, but that doesn't mean we're happy. Those family photos with those fake smiles. The fake flowers all over the house. My stepmom being all nice—that's fake too. Things aren't always like they seem." Ethan gets quiet. Then he adds, "There's a lot you don't know about me."

I say, "There's a lot you don't know about me too."

We both look at each other. Neither of us wanting to say anything first. Then we both kinda laugh.

"Come on," Ethan says. "Let's check out my comic collection."

"Finally," I say, joking.

Then we both laugh more.

FREE LUNCH

The first day back at school, everyone is talking about all the amazing presents they got and all the cool vacations they took. I didn't get any big presents or go anywhere fancy. But I'm OK with that. I don't have to love it, but I don't have to hate it either.

The first few classes drag by, but I'm excited for lunch, so Ethan and I can catch up. When I get in the lunch line, I know what's going to happen. Rather than get mad or ashamed, I just try to own it. It's not easy, but it is what it is.

When I get to the cashier, I don't hurry her, or yell at her, or get annoyed or frustrated. I just say, "I'm in the Free Lunch Program. My name's Rex Ogle."

The old woman licks her fingers and thumbs through the pages in the red folder. For the first time, I see her nametag. I wonder if she's always worn it. She probably has, and I feel a little bad about that. All those times I wanted her to memorize my name and I never bothered to learn hers. Her name is Peggy.

I ask, "How were your holidays, Peggy?"

She smiles. "Oh, they were lovely. Thanks for asking."

Peggy pencils in a little checkmark in the red folder, and says, "Did you have a good New Year?"

I nod. I did. And I'm ready for my fresh start.

AUTHOR'S NOTE

just finished writing the story you've just finished reading. I feel exhausted and sad and a little sick to my stomach. (Don't worry, I'm not going to puke on you.) The reason I feel like I'm about to vomit, or maybe just burst into tears, is because everything that happened in this book happened to me in real life. Every laugh, every lunch, and every punch that you've read about is the result of an emotional deep dive into my past.

Like most children entering sixth grade, I was focused on friends and grades and locker combinations. But I was also worried about other things: where I'd get my next meal, what mood my mom or stepdad might be in when I came home from school, and when other kids would finally discover my darkest secret—that I was poor.

I was beyond terrified of my peers knowing that my parents—and by proxy, me—were on welfare, using food stamps and living in government-subsidized housing. Along with living under the federal poverty line, I also dealt with verbal and physical abuse on a regular basis. I hated my life and I hated myself. I didn't want people to know that my family was scraping the bottom of the barrel, because I believed being poor meant being *less-than*. And I was deeply ashamed for it. And worse, it made me feel completely alone.

As an adult, I finally accepted that my shame was misplaced, and that I was hardly the only one. Right now in the United States, 43.1 million people are living in a state of poverty. Of that total, more than 14.5 million are children under the age of eighteen. According to the US Census Bureau, people under the age of eighteen have a higher poverty rate than those in any other age group. That's nearly 1 out of 5 children in America living in a state of poverty.

And that statistic doesn't even account for those around the globe who also suffer financial hardship—many of them far worse than anything I experienced.

The worst part of living like this is thinking as I did—that I was alone, that I was shameful, and that I had less worth because of the situations into which I was born. But that couldn't be further from the truth.

No child should feel alone. Or ashamed. Or worthless. They need to know that their circumstances are *not* their fault.

As an author, I tried not to write about my childhood for a very long time. In truth, I actively avoided it. It was simply too painful to revisit. But in recent years, I realized that little has changed in our national and global socioeconomic systems. In many ways, they have gotten worse. That revelation made me feel like I needed to write this story. I wrote *Free Lunch* because I honestly believe it's an important story to share. Not just to share a lived experience and to let others know they are not alone, but to offer a voice of camaraderie to those young readers who might desperately need it.

Yes, life can be hard—sometimes insanely, terrifyingly, impossibly hard. For some, it even ends tragically. But life can also be beautiful, wonderful, and full of joy. More often than not, life simply swings back and forth between the bad and the good.

If you are having a hard time, my advice is simple: Hang in there. Give it time. And stay strong. No matter how bad your circumstances may seem, things can change. And until they do, no one can take away your most powerful gift—your ability to hope for the better.

ACKNOWLEDGMENTS

My first and biggest thanks goes to my Abuela. As far back as I can remember, she has always been there for me in one capacity or another. Coming from true poverty in Mexico, she insists that education is the only path to success. Over the years, she has bought me an endless number of pens, pencils, notepads, books, and computers. She has never stopped encouraging me. Thank you, Abuela.

I also want to extend my gratitude to my editor and publisher, Simon Boughton, who believed in my story enough to take a chance on it. To Véronique Sweet, who led Simon to me. To Noah Michelson, who let me write a piece for the *Huffington Post* that gave me the confidence I needed in nonfiction. And to Brent Taylor, the first agent who made me feel like a real author.

A heartfelt thanks to Tad Carpenter for the truly epic and beautiful book cover.

Warm literary hugs go to the entire team at Norton who helped bring this book to life, including (but not limited to) Kristin Allard for all the extra stuff, Laura Goldin, the copyeditors who kept me from looking dumb, and the publicity and marketing teams for getting me out there. Also, to the sales reps for putting my story on shelves, to the book buyers for taking a chance, and to the booksellers for all that you do. And an extra special thanks to the librarians and the teachers who are always providing hope to children, simply by sharing stories.

As for those who know me best:

To my dog, Toby, who brings me endless joy.

To my friends (especially Joe and RJ) who made me laugh when I needed it.

To my partner, Mark, who graciously supports every word I write, hugs me when I fall apart after working on the really hard stuff, and continues to teach me that even broken people deserve love, can find love, and can keep love healthy—if they put in the effort.

And to my sister, M, who has always been by my side.

AUTHOR Q&A

In the book, Rex spends a lot of time thinking about and describing food. What was your favorite food when you were in sixth grade? What's your favorite food now?

Crunchy tacos! Perhaps it's the Texan in me, but I could have eaten tacos every single day—as long as there weren't any tomatoes on them. (I love salsa but hate tomatoes. Go figure!) Mom never cooked, but sometimes we stopped by Taco Bell to get a taco six-pack for the family.

Honorable mentions go out to fried mozzarella sticks, ice cream, and cake. Those were all luxuries, but when I had them, I couldn't have been happier.

As an adult, I still love tacos. I make myself tacos a few times a month. The best part? I'm allowed to eat as many as I want. ☺

What's your favorite comic book series and do you have a favorite superhero? Why?

X-Men all the way! As you read in the book, my best friend introduced me to the *Uncanny X-Men* and *New Mutants*, and I immediately fell in love. They had amazing super powers and went on incredible adventures around the world (and in space!), but the reason I kept going back was because they protected a world that feared and hated them.

At the time, I felt like I was hated too—by kids at school and certain members of my family. I had an especially confusing relationship with my mom, yet I still wanted to help her. I can't count the number of times I went to sleep wishing for superpowers, thinking if I had them, maybe I could help others, and myself.

My favorite superhero as a kid is still my favorite superhero now. Her name is Illyana Rasputin, a.k.a. Magik. She teleports through time and space. I always wanted her powers so I could get away from my life. But the real reason I identified with her is she spent her childhood lost in a demonic realm called Limbo. Even though she lived through horrible things, she stayed strong and kept fighting to be a good person. I really looked up to her for that.

When did you know you wanted to write?

When I was younger, I desperately wanted to be an artist like Gustav Klimt or Alphonse Mucha or Jim Lee or Chris Bachalo. I took every art class my school offered, and I tried so so so so so so hard. But I was never very good. One day, an art teacher asked me about the inspiration for my pieces. I started in on this very long, very in-depth high-fantasy story. My teacher listened, smiled, and said, "That's quite an imagination—have you ever thought about writing down your ideas?" She even let me write in art class. Once I started writing, I couldn't stop.

Why did you decide to tell the specific and difficult story of your sixth grade experience?

As a kid, I often looked for books about people like me— broke, scared, dealing with heavy stuff at home . . . I couldn't find anything that spoke about those topics. That reinforced my feelings about being embarrassed of who I was and where I came from. As a young writer, I didn't want people knowing about my childhood, so I kept that stuff to myself.

One day, when I was riding on the subway in New York City, I saw a little girl tug on her mom's sleeve and heard her say, "I'm hungry." Her mom hugged her, but didn't say anything. I didn't know their situation, but it struck me that my story needed to be shared. I wanted other kids to know that it's okay to be hungry. That they are not alone. And there is hope.

You could have written a fictionalized version of this story, but you chose to write it as a memoir. Why?

To be honest, the first time I tried to write this story, I positioned it as a comedy. I kept trying to make a joke about being poor, about having a difficult home life. It felt wrong though, like I was laughing at myself. But I kept thinking, "No one wants to read a sad story." Luckily, a close friend kept saying, "People don't always need to laugh. Sometimes, it's okay to hurt."

In my personal life, I believe "Honesty is the best policy." So I applied that to my writing. It took me a long time to write the first draft, almost two years, because it was uncomfortable, and made me deeply sad to revisit those memories. When I was finished though, I was really happy with what I'd written.

Was there anything you decided to leave out?

There were quite a few bits I left out. They weren't essential to tell this story. For example, there were a lot more fights between my stepdad, my mom, and me. Some were just yelling. Some of them were more violent. But I don't think I needed to include every battle to convey what I lived through. I wanted to give a full picture of my life. That meant including home, school, family, friendships, and so on.

There was one story thread—a very important one in the development of who I am as a person—that I pulled from the book entirely (except for a single mention). I wanted to include it, but decided it needed more attention. In that regard, it's become the central focus for my next project.

What were some of your favorite books in middle school? What are your favorites now?

As you know, I loved *X-Men* and *New Mutants*. But I also was going through a "classics" phase, reading titles like *A Wrinkle in Time*, *The Giver*, *Hatchet*, and *Little Women*. This was also around the time that I discovered *The Chronicles of Narnia*, which I adored. I was also reading a lot of *Hardy*

Boys and R.L. Stine's *Fear Street* series. I really began to love horror and fantasy, which led me back to more classics, like Bram Stoker's *Dracula* and Mary Shelley's *Frankenstein*. From there, I started reading Stephen King. It was a little too mature for me at the time, but I think it helped offer me perspective on my own life.

I'm still an avid reader, devouring everything from adult to children's titles. And I'm still reading a ton of comics—some of the most creative and unique stories are being created in that space by people like Jonathan Hickman, Rick Remender, and Brian K. Vaughan. I'm absolutely thrilled to see so many middle-grade graphic novels taking root, so I go after every title by folks like Noelle Stevenson, Raina Telgemeier, Mariko Tamaki, and Jeffrey Brown (to name just a few). I also read a lot of prose, but I skew toward young adult. My favorites include Jason Reynolds and his *Track* series, as well as *Harry Potter* and (this should be no surprise) *The Hunger Games*.

When you aren't writing, what are some things you like to do?

But I'm always writing! (Or reading.) Haha. When I take the occasional break, I really enjoy hiking with my friends and my dog. I usually go on big group nature meets once a week. We also like to play video games and board games. I think it's a nice way to laugh with your friends and have an adventure that gets you outside of your head. To relax, I also like to cook. Growing up, we ate a lot of junk food and fast food. As I got older, I realized I needed to take better care of my body. So I do my own shopping and try to balance my diet with healthy salads and organic treats. Though I still have a weakness for cookies and cake.

If you could say one thing to everyone who reads your book, what would it be?

"If your story is similar to mine—or even if it's not, whatever you're going through—YOU ARE NOT ALONE." As a child, I always felt I was. Sometimes I still feel that way. It's the worst feeling in the world. But none of us are truly alone. There are people and services that can help us. Sometimes we just have to reach out. I'd also add, "It is okay to live under the poverty line. It doesn't make you less than others. It just makes you different. And different is okay." The stigma of being poor in our country can be daunting. But no child should feel like they have less worth because of the situation they were born into.

What's it like to know this personal story of yours is out there for anyone to read?

It's both super scary and super exciting to have my story in the public eye. My one true hope is that it helps someone—even if it's just a handful of people—and lets them know they are not alone, and it's okay to be poor. It does not define you.

The first part of sixth grade was a very tough time for Rex. When and why did things start to get any easier for him?

There was no single defining moment, but I suspect it's when I realized I had to stop focusing on all the things I *didn't* have, and started focusing on all the things I *did* have. I had a roof over my head, I had clothes, and I had food—even if it wasn't always much. That's more than a lot of people have, and so I tried to be grateful for it. Of course, it was easy to forget these big revelations when I wanted to look cool in front of others.

Do you think there's such a thing as a free lunch?

That's a really good question. The first part of me wants to say, "Nothing's free!" But I think that's the ghost of my old self. Over the course of my lifetime, I've been treated to many meals and treated others to meals as well, and for no reason. It wasn't because I wanted anything. Sometimes, friendship and kind conversation is enough to want to share a meal with someone.

Can you tell us more about Rex and Ethan's friendship? How did they help each other?

I can't speak for Ethan, but for me, that friendship was invaluable. He taught me what true friendship was. It wasn't about wearing the right clothes or saying the right things.

It was about just being true to myself. We read comics, we talked about philosophy, geeked out over sci-fi. (He was a *Star Trek* fan, while I loved *Star Wars*.) Ethan didn't judge me—which is an amazing trait in someone so young. In turn, he taught me to be less judgmental of others and of myself.

It's been a number of years since you were a middle schooler. Do you think it's any easier to navigate sixth grade today than it was for you? Do you think it might be harder?

It's definitely not easier! I think middle school will always be a hard time for people. There's so much to juggle—school, homework, friends, family—not to mention our bodies and minds are changing rapidly. If anything, it's probably harder to be a middle schooler now. I suspect technology and social media make it easier to connect but also easier to stay at home rather than spend time with people IRL. Plus, it steals some key elements of privacy. Kids can be cruel, and social media makes it easier for bullies if they want to embarrass you or say hurtful things. I imagine if *Free Lunch* took place today, my story would already be online whether I wanted it to be or not!

Do you have a favorite scene in the book? Why is it your favorite?

There are two chapters that stand out to me. The first is "Bruises." It's definitely one of the darker chapters, but it felt like such a perfect snapshot of my childhood. The walk home from school, the superstition about stepping on a crack, and my concern over a mother who didn't seem so concerned about me. And then there's the moment in her room. That revelation of the lack of color in her life was so depressing and upsetting to me as a boy. It has always haunted me.

My second favorite scene is much happier, in "Christmas Tree." It was one of the first times that my family felt normal. Out shopping for trees, smelling the different kinds, trying to decide which has the perfect shape. And of course my stepdad's "pull my finger" gag backfiring. My editor wasn't a fan of that scene, but I had to keep it in because it's one of those moments that brought me so much laughter for years to come. I think it's good to remember the bad with the good and the good with the bad. Life is rarely completely one or the other, so it's good to embrace both.

Are you working on any new books or articles?

I am working on a few different projects. Most of my them are lighter in tone, or steeped in fantasy or science fiction. I write a lot of graphic novels (under various "pen names") too. But the one I'm most proud of is something of a sequel to *Free Lunch*. It's called *Punching Bag*, and it takes a closer look at domestic violence. Abuse is a hard subject and one that's not easy to talk about, especially for younger readers—which makes it feel even more important to me now. Statistics show that women and children are exposed to domestic violence more frequently than most would think.

It's horrifying to see the numbers. And so I truly believe it's another important story to tell.

Do you have any favorite writing advice or tips to share?

Don't give up! Haha. I say that because writing is definitely something you have to commit to. Especially if you want to write a whole book. What I've learned over the years is that writing is like training for a marathon. You don't wake up one day suddenly able to run twenty-six miles. You have to practice and train. That means you start small. Maybe run half a mile. Then a full mile. Then two miles. You have to build up to running long distances. But if you keep it up, and you work hard at it, then before you know it, you'll have written a whole book. And if you're anything like me, once you've finished your first, you'll be excited to start your second!

DISCUSSION GUIDE

1. In "Coupons," Rex feels bad for the wonky shopping cart at the store and decides to use it. Why does he make that choice?

2. What does Rex mean when he says in "Coupons," "But for some reason, things cost a whole lot more when you're poor?"

3. Why does Rex's English teacher, Mrs. Winstead, jump to the conclusion that he can't be reading a 1,000-page novel? What does it show us about her?

4. Why do you think Rex likes to read stories about the end of the world ("Free Reading")?

5. In "White Rabbit" why does Rex hide his action figures from Benny's older brother? Why might he like hanging out with Benny, who is two years younger and plays with toys?

6. Rex wonders if he's a rabbit or a snake in "White Rabbit." Which do you think he is? Do you agree with him that most kids are rabbits? Why?

7. What do you think about Rex's mother's argument that lying about bad service is okay because she's getting free meals from mega-rich fast food companies ("Fast Food")?

8. Why do you think Rex is so bothered by the wasp that can't find its way out of the apartment ("Bugs")?

9. Rex spends a lot of his time taking care of his little brother, Ford, and has a lot of responsibility for him, which he takes seriously. Do you think there are ways that Ford also takes care of Rex? What are some good moments that they share together?

10. Food plays a major role in this story. Why is that? What did you notice about Rex's descriptions of food?

11. In "Superheroes," Ethan asks Rex, "But if the good guys kill, what's the difference between them and the evil people?" How would you answer Ethan?

12. In "Turkey," Rex says about his mother, "Her insanity is contagious." What do you think he means when he says this?

13. Have you ever had an adult—a teacher, a friend's parent—judge you by your appearance? What does that feel like? In "Spelling," Rex finds a constructive but direct way to express his frustration with Mrs. Winstead's assumptions about him. Why do you think he forgives Mrs. Winstead so quickly after she apologizes?

14. Rex's mother always seems to be cleaning, whether it's vacuuming, doing the laundry and ironing, or scrubbing the kitchen. What does that show us about her? Rex thinks she loves cleaning and hates germs. Why else might she be cleaning?

15. Why do you think Ethan befriends Rex? How are he and Rex different? And what do they have in common ("Christmas Tree")?

16. Rex spends most of the book worrying about everything he doesn't have, whether it's clothes, food, or loving parents. Before he receives his present on Christmas morning, though, he decides to focus on what he does have. How might it help Rex in the future?

17. Rex has a complicated relationship with his stepfather, Sam. Why do you think Sam gives Rex the surprise Christmas present? What does it mean to Rex?

18. Abuela doesn't appear very often in the story, but she is still an important character. What is her influence on Rex? How does she affect him even when she's not with him?

19. By the end of the story, which character has changed the most?

20. "There's no such thing as a free lunch" is a common saying. What do you think that means? Do you think Rex feels the Free Lunch Program at school is really free?

WRITING GUIDE

Life can be fantastic, filled with fun and laughter, but it can also be difficult and overwhelming. Whatever your life is like, you might try writing about it. Changing thoughts into words, and words into stories, can help life feel a little lighter. I know when I write, things start to make a little more sense.

Writing is about organizing your feelings and taking a moment to reflect. It's not always easy to write down the bad stuff. But after I do, I always feel better, and it's good to get things out of your system. Here are some tips on writing your own stories about what's going on in your life.

WHAT DO YOU WANT TO WRITE ABOUT?

Maybe you want to write about something bad that happened to you in the past, or something happy that happened to you today. Maybe you simply want to share your hopes for something that will happen in the future. There's no wrong answer here.

HOW DO YOU WANT TO WRITE YOUR STORY?

Next, you need to decide how you want to write. Do you want to write in poetry? Or in prose? Do you want the story to be from your point of view, or do you want to tell the story from a third-person perspective? Remember, this is *your* story. You make the rules!

WHERE (AND WHEN) DOES THIS STORY TAKE PLACE?

This is an important one because you want your reader to "see" the setting when they read your words. If the story takes place on the beach, describe the sand and the salt in the air. If it takes place in space, make sure your hero wears a spacesuit. If it takes place during cowboy times, maybe your hero will ride a horse.

WHAT IS THE BEGINNING, MIDDLE, AND END OF YOUR STORY?

If this is a long story, you might want to imagine what the "movie trailer" would look like. Then write down those ideas. Is there lots of action? Or is this more of a heartfelt story? Map what happens from start to finish.

WRITE AN OUTLINE!

This might be the most important bit of advice I can offer. If you write an outline first, it'll help you along the way, because you'll know which direction you're going. The more work you do earlier, the less you have to do later.

START WRITING!

Now it's time to start writing. This part will take the longest, but don't rush it, and don't stress over every single word and sentence. If it helps, just let it all out and write down everything.

BE HONEST.

This might seem easy, but it can actually be very hard. The first time I tried to write my story, I wanted to be the nicest person in the book. But that wasn't accurate. To be honest, I had to show my character being a jerk sometimes. Sometimes bad people are nice, and sometimes nice people are bad. No one is 100 percent evil or 100 percent good. The truth lies somewhere in the middle.

THE FIVE SENSES.

When you're writing any story, you want to paint a picture for the reader. The best way to do that is to address the five senses. If your main character goes into a garden, what does it smell like? How does the sun feel on their skin? Are there any sounds? The more sensory information you can add, the more realistic it will be for the reader.

WHEN YOU'RE DONE . . . TAKE A BREAK!

Once you have written your story, give yourself some time off. Pat yourself on the back and treat yourself to something fun. When you're ready, come back to it. It'll be waiting for you.

REVISE.

This is the place where you read it and make corrections. First, do a creative edit. That means, focus on the story and the way you wrote it. Does each sentence (and paragraph) make sense? Are you saying what you meant to say? Are there any details you could add to make the story feel deeper, or more realistic?

Once you do that, take one more pass, and check for spelling errors and punctuation mistakes. If you find a lot, don't beat yourself up. When I'm writing, I still confuse *they're*, *there*, and *their* sometimes. A lot of times I write so fast, I make silly spelling errors. No writer is perfect.

DON'T BE AFRAID OF REJECTION.

Sharing your writing might be the scariest part of the whole process. It's okay to be nervous. If you don't want to share it, if you want to keep it private, that's okay too. Some stories can be just for you. If you do decide to share your work, remember that hard times are not only tough to write about; they can be tough to read about, too, especially for people who lived through them. The most important thing is to pick a reader you trust, and one you feel safe with. That might not be a family member (it certainly wouldn't have been for me), so please be careful about this. Your safety is the most important thing!

BE OPEN TO NOTES.

If you do share, then be ready to hear people's thoughts and opinions. Some people may offer "constructive criticism," which means they are being critical to be helpful. Their advice might be terrible, but it might also be great. Just stay open to new ideas. Remember, some people will love your story, and others won't, and that's okay.

FINAL PIECE OF ADVICE.

If you want to know the key to being a great writer, it's really quite simple: **READ, READ, READ!** The more you read other people's books, the better you'll learn to craft and shape your own stories. After all, the best writers are great readers.

BEST OF LUCK,

REX OGLE

RESOURCES

If you or someone you know is experiencing hunger, depression, anxiety, or domestic violence, please know that *you are not alone*, and *there is help*. There are people who are trained to listen without judgment and to connect you with resources or information you need.

As of the date of this writing, the services listed below are free and are available 24 hours a day, 7 days a week, 365 days a year. The information I've included here comes from the internet (meaning that I don't have personal experience with each of these organizations and can't guarantee results) but I hope this list is a helpful starting place.

Hunger Free America

Resource for individuals or families seeking information on how to obtain food, and connects callers with emergency food providers in their community, assistance programs, and social services.
1-866-3-HUNGRY (for English)
1-877-8-HAMBRE (for Spanish)

www.hungerfreeamerica.org

www.hungerfreeamerica.org/food-map

Substance Abuse and Mental Health Services Administration

Provides free, confidential, 24/7 services for individuals or families facing mental and/or substance use disorders.

1-800-662-HELP (4357)

www.samhsa.gov/find-help/national-helpline

National Suicide Prevention Lifeline

Provides 24/7, free, and confidential support to people in emotional distress or suicide crisis.

1-800-273-8255

www.suicidepreventionlifeline.org

National Domestic Violence Hotline

Provides lifesaving tools and immediate support to enable victims to find safety and live lives free of abuse.

1-800-799-SAFE (7233)

www.thehotline.org